★ ★ ★ ★ WHOSE RIGHT IS IT? ★ ★ ★ ★

THE FOURTEENTH AMENDMENT

—— AND THE ——

FIGHT FOR EQUALITY

Hana Bajramovic

HENRY HOLT AND COMPANY
NEW YORK

Henry Holt and Company, *Publishers since 1866*
Henry Holt® is a registered trademark of Macmillan Publishing Group, LLC
120 Broadway, New York, NY 10271 • mackids.com

Our books may be purchased in bulk for promotional, educational, or business use.
Please contact your local bookseller or the Macmillan Corporate and Premium Sales Department
at (800) 221-7945 ext. 5442 or by email at MacmillanSpecialMarkets@macmillan.com.

Library of Congress Cataloging-in-Publication Data is available.

First edition, 2024
Book design by Maria W. Jenson
Printed in the United States of America by BVG, Fairfield, Pennsylvania

ISBN 978-1-250-22527-6
1 3 5 7 9 10 8 6 4 2

To my parents

★ ★ ★ ★ ★ ★ ★ Contents ★ ★ ★ ★ ★ ★ ★

THE FOURTEENTH AMENDMENT

Section 1. All persons born or naturalized in the United States, and subject to the jurisdiction thereof, are citizens of the United States and of the State wherein they reside. No State shall make or enforce any law which shall abridge the privileges or immunities of citizens of the United States; nor shall any State deprive any person of life, liberty, or property, without due process of law; nor deny to any person within its jurisdiction the equal protection of the laws.

Section 2. Representatives shall be apportioned among the several States according to their respective numbers, counting the whole number of persons in each State, excluding Indians not taxed. But when the right to vote at any election for the choice of electors for President and Vice-President of the United States, Representatives in Congress, the Executive and Judicial officers of a State, or the members of the Legislature thereof, is denied to any of the male inhabitants of such State, being twenty-one years of age,* and citizens of the United States, or in any way abridged, except for participation in rebellion, or other crime, the basis of representation therein shall be reduced in the proportion which the number

---

* In 1971, the voting age was lowered to eighteen by the Twenty-Sixth Amendment.

of such male citizens shall bear to the whole number of male citizens twenty-one years of age in such State.

Section 3. No person shall be a Senator or Representative in Congress, or elector of President and Vice-President, or hold any office, civil or military, under the United States, or under any State, who, having previously taken an oath, as a member of Congress, or as an officer of the United States, or as a member of any State legislature, or as an executive or judicial officer of any State, to support the Constitution of the United States, shall have engaged in insurrection or rebellion against the same, or given aid or comfort to the enemies thereof. But Congress may by a vote of two-thirds of each House, remove such disability.

Section 4. The validity of the public debt of the United States, authorized by law, including debts incurred for payment of pensions and bounties for services in suppressing insurrection or rebellion, shall not be questioned. But neither the United States nor any State shall assume or pay any debt or obligation incurred in aid of insurrection or rebellion against the United States, or any claim for the loss or emancipation of any slave; but all such debts, obligations and claims shall be held illegal and void.

Section 5. The Congress shall have the power to enforce, by appropriate legislation, the provisions of this article.

★ ★ ★ ★ ★ ★ **Introduction** ★ ★ ★ ★ ★

What does it mean to be a "citizen" of the United States?

For Dred Scott, a Black man born around 1799, citizenship was denied to him because he was enslaved.

In the late 1890s, Wong Kim Ark's citizenship was called into question—even though he was born in the United States—simply because his parents were Chinese subjects.

Myra Bradwell, a white woman seeking to become a lawyer in 1869, may have been a citizen, but the rights of citizenship were different for her because of her gender.

For Mildred and Richard Loving, an interracial couple who married in 1958, and Jim Obergefell and John Arthur, two men who married in 2013, basic rights of citizenship could be denied to them because of their race and sexual orientation, respectively.

Throughout U.S. history—up to and including today—the meaning of citizenship has been intertwined with elements of identity like race, gender, immigration status, and sexual orientation. Who we are has determined what rights we are granted.

The Fourteenth Amendment, sometimes referred to as the "equality amendment," was passed after the Civil War to address one aspect of this unfairness: race discrimination. In part I of this book, we'll look at how the amendment was drafted and the issues it sought to address. In part II, we'll see how the Supreme Court interpreted the rights granted by the amendment in the years following its passage. And in part III, we'll learn how the Fourteenth

Amendment grew to encompass gender discrimination, immigrants' rights, and LGBTQ+ rights, and how the amendment today is the basis of hot-button political issues like abortion access, affirmative action, and marriage equality.

The Fourteenth Amendment tells the story of the fight for equality in the United States, but it also shows us the limits of law. Dred Scott, Wong Kim Ark, Myra Bradwell, Mildred and Richard Loving, Jim Obergefell, and John Arthur all argued in court that the Fourteenth Amendment protected their rights. Some of their cases were successful; others weren't. In none of their cases, however, did the law provide a full solution.

Dred Scott and his family found their freedom not through the courts, but because of public outcry. When Myra Bradwell eventually received her law license, it was not because of her Supreme Court case; to the contrary, three of the justices wrote that the "paramount destiny" of a woman is "to fulfill the noble and benign offices of wife and mother." Even though the Supreme Court said Wong Kim Ark was a citizen, he was arrested in Texas in 1901 for being a "Chinese person" living "illegally" in the United States. And while marriage can no longer be limited by race or sexual orientation, those Supreme Court decisions are on shaky footing.

Despite all this—or perhaps because of it—the Fourteenth Amendment may be the most important amendment on the list. Though it never fully achieved its aims, the story of the Fourteenth Amendment and the many people who fought for its ideals shows us how we can continue to work toward true equality.

LAW SCHOOL 101

What Is an Amendment to the Constitution?

An amendment is a change to the Constitution. Since the Constitution was ratified (approved), it has been amended twenty-seven times. A constitutional amendment is different from an act, which is a law passed by Congress or state legislatures. We'll learn later about how it's much harder to get an amendment ratified than it is to get a law passed.

What Is the Bill of Rights?

The Bill of Rights refers to the first ten amendments to the Constitution. These amendments guarantee certain rights, like free speech (First Amendment) or a speedy trial in criminal cases (Sixth Amendment). We'll learn a lot more about these specific rights later on in this book.

What Is Congress?

Congress is the legislative (lawmaking) branch of the federal (national) government. It's made up of the House of Representatives and the Senate. Each state sends two senators to Congress and a certain number of representatives based on its population.

Who Decides What a Law Means?

After laws are passed, they are interpreted by courts. People may sue, arguing that their rights under a certain law have been violated—meaning that someone harmed them in a way that the law was supposed to prevent. The person who sues is called the plaintiff, and the person being sued is called the defendant. The lawsuit, called a case, is named after these two parties: *Plaintiff v. Defendant.*

Courts then decide whether the particular facts of the case amount to a violation of the law. So for example, imagine a law said, "The government must compensate you appropriately when it takes your property." If the government took your land to make a public park and paid you a few thousand dollars, you might sue, arguing that your land was worth much more than that. The court that decided your case would help interpret what it meant for compensation to be "appropriate." The court's opinion would become case law, which has the same effect as a law passed by Congress or a state legislature.

Certain cases are decided by more than one judge. In these instances, the judges might disagree on how the case should come out. The majority opinion becomes the binding case law, and the judges who disagree write what are known as dissents, which are not binding. (When something is binding, that means it has the force of law.) Judges who support the majority decision but for different reasons can write concurring opinions, which are also not binding.

The section of the court's majority decision that rules on the specific issue the court was asked to decide is known as that opinion's holding. You can think of an opinion's holding as the legal principle you should draw from the case.

What Different Federal Courts Are There?

There are three levels of courts in the federal system: ninety-four district courts, thirteen courts of appeals, and the one and only U.S. Supreme Court. (State court systems are structured similarly, as we'll learn later on.)

To bring a federal lawsuit, you first file your case in a district court. If you lose your case in the district court and want to challenge the decision, you file a brief with the court of appeals explaining where the district court went wrong.

If you lose in the court of appeals, you might then ask the Supreme Court to hear your case. This is called filing a petition for a writ of certiorari, or a cert petition.

In most situations, the Supreme Court can decide whether or not it wants to hear your case. Four of the justices (judges) on the court must vote to take a case for it to be heard by the Supreme Court. Of the seven to eight thousand cert petitions filed each year, the court takes only about eighty—so when a case gets to the Supreme Court, you know it's serious.

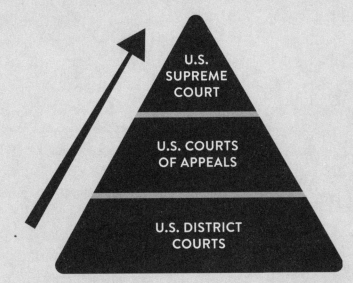

Court levels in the federal system

Who Chooses U.S. Supreme Court Justices?

Supreme Court justices are nominated by the president then in power and approved by the Senate. We'll learn throughout this text that even though the justices are supposed to stay out of politics, they often have political views that reflect the party of the president who nominated them.

Part I

THE CONSTITUTION

The Amendment That Never Was

The Fourteenth Amendment was ratified in 1868, but its story starts in the late 1700s, back when the Constitution and the Bill of Rights were being drafted. The Bill of Rights has ten amendments in it—a nice, round number. It might seem like that was intentional, but it wasn't.

In fact, James Madison initially proposed nine amendments, including one about state governments that he considered the most important of all. Most lawmakers at the time of the founding viewed the federal government as the biggest threat to individual rights. Madison, however, believed state governments were also "liable to attack" their inhabitants' "invaluable privileges." He proposed an amendment that he believed would help solve that problem, but it didn't make the final cut.

Before we explore the issues that motivated the drafters of the Fourteenth Amendment, we must first understand Madison's lost amendment and the story it tells about the relationship between the federal government and the states—what's called federalism.

FEDERALISM

Have you ever heard your parents mention that they have to pay both state and federal taxes? Or have you noticed that some laws are state laws, passed by state governments, while other laws are federal laws, passed by Congress? State and federal governments share power and work in parallel; they each have their own laws, constitutions, and court systems. The complicated interplay between state and federal governments is known as federalism.

The Constitution spells out specific powers belonging to the federal government. These include the right to regulate goods and services that travel between states (known as interstate commerce), the right to declare war, and the right to impose taxes. All governmental powers that are not assigned to the federal government, such as the power to make laws for public safety and to create school systems, belong to the states. And if state and federal laws conflict, Article VI of the Constitution—the supremacy clause—says that you have to follow the federal law.

States also have their own constitutions, separate and apart from the federal Constitution. State constitutions might look a lot like the U.S. Constitution, but they don't have to.

There are also separate state and federal courts. Federal courts can hear only certain sorts of cases: cases about federal laws and cases between citizens of different states. This separation developed because federal courts were seen as better able to interpret federal law and less likely to favor citizens of one state over another. State courts, on the other hand, have what's called general jurisdiction, which means they can hear all sorts of cases.

This messy relationship between state and federal governments is a major feature of American government. From the 1700s to today, states and the federal government have been in a tug-of-war for power—because federalism is, in essence, a compromise. Sometimes states are in control; sometimes the federal government is. Throughout this book—and this chapter in particular—the concept of federalism will arise and intersect with issues of racism and equality.

The Constitution and State Power

In 1781, late in the Revolutionary War and a century before the Fourteenth Amendment became law, America ratified its first constitution: the Articles of Confederation and Perpetual Union. The Articles were an agreement between the thirteen original states that created a central government but still respected the independence of the states. Despite the name, the Articles of Confederation and Perpetual Union were short-lived.

The Articles gave the national government very little power; there was no president, and the Congress, called the "Congress of the Confederation," was a single legislature (which means it did not have both a Senate and a House of Representatives as it does today). Under the Articles, states were operating like their own little countries.

The Articles proved to be a problem when the end of the Revolutionary War came around. "The long, hard war had devastated the American economy," historian Alan Taylor explains. He continues:

> Roaming armies and frontier raiders uprooted thousands
> of people by destroying their farms, plantations, and towns.
> At least 25,000 Americans died in military service, usually
> of disease . . . British warships disrupted the export trade
> essential to prosperity. Economic historians find a 30 percent
> decline in national income between 1774 and 1790: a
> decline which they characterize as "America's greatest income
> slump ever," and an "economic disaster."

The federal government was too weak to fix these economic woes. It needed "new powers to levy taxes and regulate interstate and foreign commerce"—which it didn't have under the Articles.

In May 1787, twelve of the thirteen original states—all but Rhode Island—sent representatives, known as delegates, to meet in Philadelphia for something called the Constitutional Convention. (Rhode Island refused to send any delegates because it didn't believe in giving the federal government more power.) At the convention, the fifty-five delegates planned to discuss how to recover from the war. Ultimately, they would draft a new constitution outlining a structure of government that they hoped would serve the nation as a whole.

All fifty-five of the delegates were white, and many of them were enslavers. "No known black people were involved in the constitutional debates preceding the adoption of the Constitution," writes lawyer and author J. Clay Smith Jr. (It's important to think about the worldview and biases of the group of people who created this document, and all the perspectives that were missing.)

Before the Constitutional Convention, James Madison had studied world governments—including ancient Greece, the Roman Empire, Switzerland, and the Netherlands—to come up with his ideal political system: a strong central government with power spread across three branches. Madison was always advocating for a stronger federal government; his time working in the Virginia state government "convinced him of the dangers inherent in the powerful state legislatures and of the weaknesses of the Articles of Confederation." By splitting the federal government into three branches—executive, legislative, and judicial—he hoped each branch would serve as a check on the power of the others.

After four months of debate at the Constitutional Convention, this three-branch form of government was adopted, and the Constitution was born.

JAMES MADISON

James Madison

James Madison was born on March 16, 1751, the oldest son of a wealthy Virginia family. He grew up on his family's plantation, where Black people were enslaved, and graduated from the College of New Jersey (now Princeton University), where he studied moral philosophy. Madison has been described by various historians as "scholarly, sickly, astute, and shy," and "weak of voice." Nevertheless, he decided to become a politician. He served in the Virginia government and joined the Continental Congress in 1780. After the Constitution was ratified, he was elected to the House of Representatives, where he drafted the Bill of Rights (more on that later). Before being elected the fourth president of the United States, he also served as secretary of state. Madison died in 1836 at the age of eighty-five.

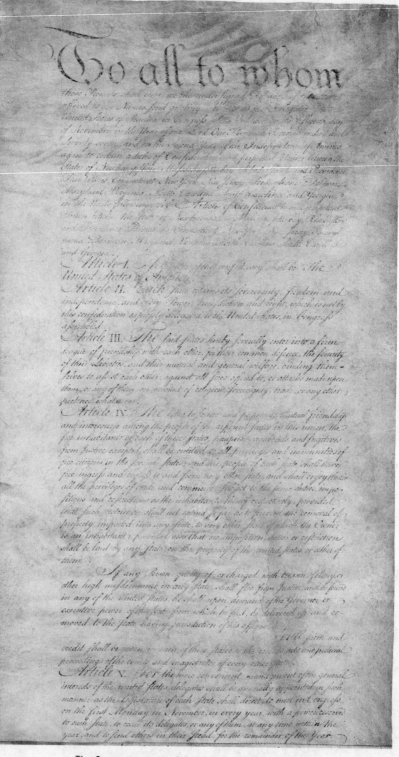

The first two pages of the Articles. Great cursive!

No state shall be represented in Congress by less than two, nor by more than seven Members; and no person shall be capable of being a delegate for more than three years in any term of six years: nor shall any person, being a delegate, be capable of holding any office under the united states, for which he, or another for his benefit receives any salary, fees or emolument of any kind.

Each state shall maintain its own delegates in a meeting of the states, and while they act as members of the committee of the states.

In determining questions in the united states, in Congress assembled, each state shall have one vote.

Freedom of speech and debate in Congress shall not be impeached or questioned in any Court, or place out of Congress, and the members of congress shall be protected in their persons from arrests and imprisonments during the time of their going to and from, and attendance on congress, except for treason, felony, or breach of the peace.

Article VI. No state without the Consent of the united states in congress assembled, shall send any embassy to, or receive any embassy from, or enter into any conference, agreement, alliance or treaty with any King prince or state; nor shall any person holding any office of profit or trust under the united states, or any of them, accept of any present, emolument, office or title of any kind whatever from any king, prince or foreign state; nor shall the united states in congress assembled, or any of them, grant any title of nobility.

No two or more states shall enter into any treaty, confederation or alliance whatever between them, without the consent of the united states in congress assembled, specifying accurately the purposes for which the same is to be entered into, and how long it shall continue.

No state shall lay any imposts or duties, which may interfere with any stipulations in treaties, entered into by the united states in congress assembled, with any king, prince or state, in pursuance of any treaties already proposed by congress, to the courts of France and Spain.

No vessels of war shall be kept up in time of peace by any state, except such number only, as shall be deemed necessary by the united states in congress assembled, for the defence of such state, or its trade; nor shall any body of forces be kept up by any state, in time of peace, except such number only, as in the judgment of the united states, in congress assembled, shall be deemed requisite to garrison the forts necessary for the defence of such state; but every state shall always keep up a well regulated and disciplined militia, sufficiently armed and accoutred, and shall provide and constantly have ready for use, in public stores, a due number of field pieces and tents, and a proper quantity of arms, ammunition and camp equipage.

No state shall engage in any war without the consent of the united states in congress assembled, unless such state be actually invaded by enemies, or shall have received certain advice of a resolution being formed by some nation of Indians to invade such state, and the danger is so imminent as not to admit of a delay, till the united states in congress assembled can be consulted: nor shall any state grant commissions to any ships or vessels of war, nor letters of marque or reprisal, except it be after a declaration of war by the united states in congress assembled, and then only against the kingdom or state and the subjects thereof, against which war has been so declared, and under such regulations as shall be established by the united states in congress assembled, unless such state be infested by pirates, in which case vessels of war may be fitted out for that occasion, and kept so long as the danger shall continue, or until the united states in congress assembled shall determine otherwise.

Madison also had a lot of ideas that his fellow Convention attendees *didn't* like. One of those ideas was the "national veto." In 1787, Madison suggested that the Constitution should let Congress veto (reject) state laws that it believed were unconstitutional. As Madison wrote to George Washington in April 1787:

> *Another happy effect of this prerogative would be its controul on the internal vicissitudes of State policy, and the aggressions of interested majorities on the rights of minorities and of individuals. The great desideratum, which has not yet been found for Republican Governments, seems to be some disinterested and dispassionate umpire in disputes between different passions and interests in the State. The majority, who alone have the right of decision, have frequently an interest, real or supposed, in abusing it. In Monarchies, the sovereign is more neutral to the interests and views of different parties; but, unfortunately, he too often forms interests of his own repugnant to those of the whole. Might not the national prerogative here suggested be found sufficiently disinterested for the decision of local questions of policy, whilst it would itself be sufficiently restrained from the pursuit of interests adverse to those of the whole Society?*

In other words, Madison explained, the national veto could help the federal government prevent states from trampling on the rights of individuals. Madison viewed the federal government as a "disinterested and dispassionate umpire" that could stop the political majorities in each state from using their power to harm the minority—just as an umpire in baseball calls balls and strikes and makes sure each side is following the rules.

The other delegates at the Constitutional Convention weren't convinced. They thought that a national veto was too drastic and that it gave the federal government entirely too much power. Keep in mind the context: The United States had just declared itself independent from England, leaving many Americans wary of putting too much power in one government and potentially creating a new monarchy. Madison was already proposing a dramatically stronger central government, and now he wanted to give that government veto power over what was happening in the states.

So the Constitution moved ahead without Madison's national veto, and in June 1788, the document became the law of the land after it was approved by three-fourths of the states.

SLAVERY IN THE CONSTITUTION

Although the Constitution doesn't ever actually use the word "slavery," it makes reference to it in several places. For example, Article I, Section 9 allowed an import tax of up to "ten dollars for each Person." (A tax is a fee charged by the government that then funds government spending.)

Article I, Section 9 also prevented Congress from banning slavery before 1808: "Migration or Importation of such Persons as any of the States now existing shall think proper to admit, shall not be prohibited by the Congress prior to the Year one thousand eight hundred and eight." This meant that states could abolish slavery if they wanted to, but Congress couldn't—at least not for a while.

In Article IV, Section 2, the Constitution said that a "Person held to Service or Labour in one State, under the Laws thereof, escaping into another" must be "delivered up on Claim of the Party to whom such Service or Labour may be due"—which meant that an enslaved person who escaped to a free state had to be returned to slavery.

What's more, Article I, Section 2 said that the number of representatives a state got in Congress would be "determined by adding to the whole Number of free Persons . . . three fifths of *all other Persons*" (people who were enslaved) (italics added). This clause dehumanized people who were enslaved by refusing to count them as full people. It also gave Southern states disproportionate power in Congress, by counting enslaved people to determine the number of representatives, even though people who were enslaved could not vote for those representatives.

In all these ways, the Constitution affirmed and protected the existence of slavery—without saying the word once.

A painting depicting the signing of the Constitution at the 1787 convention in Philadelphia (by John Henry Hintermeister, 1925)

The Bill of Rights and the Lost Fourteenth

When it was first presented to the states for their approval, the Constitution didn't contain a bill of rights; it focused instead on how the federal government would run. States had their own constitutions with their own bills of rights, so the framers didn't think a national one was necessary. But many states were unhappy with this absence—it meant the Constitution didn't protect individual rights against the power of the federal government. Indeed, some states said they'd ratify the Constitution only if the framers promised to later add a bill of rights.

The framers made that promise, and a year after the Constitution's ratification, James Madison proposed a set of amendments that were similar to the bills of rights in many state constitutions. After numerous additions, deletions, and revisions from the House and Senate, ten amendments were ratified by the states and became the official Bill of Rights in the U.S. Constitution.

THE BILL OF RIGHTS

	Amendment	Translation
I	Congress shall make no law respecting an establishment of religion, or prohibiting the free exercise thereof; or abridging the freedom of speech, or of the press; or the right of the people peaceably to assemble, and to petition the Government for a redress of grievances.	The First Amendment is chock-full of rights. First, it says that the government can't favor any particular religion. This clause, called the establishment clause, often comes into play when local governments put up Christmas displays around the holidays. The U.S. Supreme Court has said that such displays are okay only if they also include items from other religions, like Jewish menorahs.

	Amendment	Translation
I (cont.)		The First Amendment also says that the government can't interfere with your religious beliefs or, in most cases, stop you from practicing your religion. This is what's known as the free exercise clause. Next, the amendment says that the government can't punish you for speaking your mind (freedom of speech) or interfere with media or news outlets (freedom of press). Of course, there are limits to this—you can't yell "Fire!" in a crowded theater because it would be a threat to public safety, and journalists can't publish things they know are lies. The First Amendment also promises freedom of assembly, which means the government can't prevent you from joining organizations, clubs, or political parties, no matter how unpopular those groups may be. And finally, the amendment says you can complain to the government when you think it's done something wrong—that's what it means to petition for a redress of your grievances.
II	A well regulated Militia, being necessary to the security of a free State, the right of the people to keep and bear Arms, shall not be infringed.	The Second Amendment means that people have the right to keep and bear guns, under some reasonable restrictions. (This amendment's history is long and complicated and is the subject of an entire other book in this series!)

	Amendment	Translation
III	No Soldier shall, in time of peace be quartered in any house, without the consent of the Owner, nor in time of war, but in a manner to be prescribed by law.	The Third Amendment says that during peacetime, soldiers aren't allowed to walk up to your house and demand that you let them stay with you. (This was more of a problem before the Revolutionary War, when British soldiers would demand that the colonists house and feed them.)
IV	The right of the people to be secure in their persons, houses, papers, and effects, against unreasonable searches and seizures, shall not be violated, and no Warrants shall issue, but upon probable cause, supported by Oath or affirmation, and particularly describing the place to be searched, and the persons or things to be seized.	The Fourth Amendment tells government officials (often police officers) that they can't stop and search you, your house, or your possessions unless they have a good reason to believe you've done something wrong. And they can't get a warrant to do so unless they explain to a judge very specifically who or what needs to be searched.
V	No person shall be held to answer for a capital, or otherwise infamous crime, unless on a presentment or indictment of a Grand Jury, except in cases arising in the land or naval forces, or in the Militia, when in actual service in time of War or public danger; nor shall any person be subject for the same offence to be twice put in jeopardy of life or limb; nor shall be compelled in any criminal case to be a witness against himself, nor be deprived of life, liberty, or property, without due process of law; nor shall private property	The Fifth Amendment protects your right to a grand jury in cases when you're accused of a felony (felonies are more serious crimes). A grand jury is a group of people who look at the evidence against you and decide whether you should be brought to trial—the idea is that people should be protected from false accusations of serious crimes and shouldn't have to go to trial at all if there isn't enough evidence.

The amendment also says that you can't be tried twice for the same crime and that you can't be forced to testify against yourself, which means you have the right to remain silent. |

	Amendment	Translation
V (cont.)	be taken for public use, without just compensation.	The amendment next says you've got a right to "due process" before the government takes away your life, liberty, or property, which means the government has to follow fair legal procedures when it punishes you or takes things from you. Finally, the amendment's takings clause says the government can't take your property unless it pays you a fair amount. This can come up, for example, when the government wants to build a highway but your house is in the way.
VI	In all criminal prosecutions, the accused shall enjoy the right to a speedy and public trial, by an impartial jury of the State and district wherein the crime shall have been committed, which district shall have been previously ascertained by law, and to be informed of the nature and cause of the accusation; to be confronted with the witnesses against him; to have compulsory process for obtaining witnesses in his favor, and to have the Assistance of Counsel for his defence.	The Sixth Amendment says that in criminal cases, you have a right to trial by jury and that trial has to be speedy—the government can't make you wait for it forever. Your trial also has to be in the same place where the crime was committed; you have to know what you were charged with; and you're entitled to question (or confront) the people who accuse you at your trial. You also have the right to a lawyer to help you defend yourself.
VII	In Suits at common law, where the value in controversy shall exceed twenty dollars, the right of trial by jury shall be preserved, and no fact tried by a jury, shall be otherwise	The Seventh Amendment says you also have a right to a jury trial when a lawsuit is brought, as long as the property involved is worth more than twenty dollars. Of course, twenty dollars was worth a lot

	Amendment	Translation
VII (cont.)	re-examined in any Court of the United States, than according to the rules of the common law.	more back then—about five hundred dollars in today's money.
VIII	Excessive bail shall not be required, nor excessive fines imposed, nor cruel and unusual punishments inflicted.	The Eighth Amendment says that if you're arrested, the judge can't set unreasonably high bail. Bail is the money you have to pay to be released while you're waiting for your trial to finish; the money is returned to you as long as you show up to all your court appearances. Fines also can't be too high, and you can't be punished in ways that are "cruel and unusual," like torture. Many people think the death penalty is cruel and unusual punishment and so should be prohibited by the Eighth Amendment, but the U.S. Supreme Court has held that it is not.
IX	The enumeration in the Constitution, of certain rights, shall not be construed to deny or disparage others retained by the people.	The Ninth Amendment reminds people that they have more rights than just those listed in the Bill of Rights.
X	The powers not delegated to the United States by the Constitution, nor prohibited by it to the States, are reserved to the States respectively, or to the people.	Finally, the Tenth Amendment explains that if the Constitution doesn't explicitly give the federal government certain powers, and doesn't explicitly prohibit states from wielding certain powers, then the powers belong to the states or to the people. These are called reserved powers.

But, as we discussed earlier, Madison initially proposed some amendments that did not make it into the final version of the Bill of Rights—one of which might be considered a precursor to the Fourteenth Amendment we know today. It was the only one of Madison's proposals that protected people from their *state* governments, not just the federal government. It read: "No State shall violate the equal rights of conscience, or the freedom of the press, or the trial by jury in criminal cases."

That in article 1st, section 10, between clauses 1 and 2, be inserted this clause, to wit:

No state shall violate the equal rights of conscience, or the freedom of the press, or the trial by jury in criminal cases.

The Lost Fourteenth

Madison proposed what we might call the "Lost Fourteenth" in order to limit what states could do to control their citizens; he worried that like the national government, state governments might also infringe on rights. "If there was any reason to restrain the Government of the United States from infringing upon these essential rights," Madison explained to Congress, "it was equally necessary that they should be secured against the State Governments." So while the Lost Fourteenth was less drastic than the national veto, it was aimed at the same problem.

Wait, wait, wait—what about the state's own constitution? Didn't we just learn that state constitutions had their own bills of rights? Why wouldn't those be enough? As Madison put it:

> *I know, in some of the State constitutions, the power of*
> *the Government is controlled by such a declaration; but*
> *others are not. I cannot see any reason against obtaining*
> *even a double security on those points; and nothing can*
> *give a more sincere proof of the attachment of those who*
> *opposed this constitution to these great and important rights,*
> *than to see them join in obtaining the security I have now*
> *proposed; because it must be admitted, on all hands, that the*
> *State Governments are as liable to attack these invaluable*
> *privileges as the General Government is, and therefore ought*
> *to be as cautiously guarded against.*

Madison was saying: While some states protected these rights in their constitutions, others didn't. And there was no harm in "double security."

Plus, if the rights were in the federal constitution, people could sue for violations in federal courts. In explaining the need for a bill of rights in general, Madison suggested that federal courts were more objective and less swayed by local interests than state courts:

> *If they are incorporated into the constitution, independent*
> *tribunals of justice will consider themselves in a peculiar*
> *manner the guardians of those rights; they will be an*
> *impenetrable bulwark against every assumption of power in*
> *the legislative or executive; they will be naturally led to resist*
> *every encroachment upon rights expressly stipulated for in the*
> *constitution by the declaration of rights.*

For these same reasons, Madison believed the Lost Fourteenth's restriction on state governments made it "the most valuable amendment in the whole list."

The House of Representatives passed the Lost Fourteenth, apparently without much discussion. One representative criticized the proposed amendment, but only mildly, arguing that it would be "much better . . . to leave the State Governments to themselves, and not to interfere with them more than we already do."

The amendment didn't fare so well in the Senate. (Before a constitutional amendment can be sent to the states for ratification, it must be passed by both chambers of Congress.) Very few notes exist from the Senate debates on the Lost Fourteenth, but as Pulitzer Prize–winning historian Jack N. Rakove explains, the Senate ultimately rejected the proposal to protect "state assemblies against national encroachment." The point of the Bill of Rights was to *limit* the power of the federal government, but the Lost Fourteenth seemed to be *increasing* the federal government's ability to control states. Much like the national veto, the Lost Fourteenth was a no go.

Madison was displeased. In a September 1789 letter to Edmund Pendleton, a Virginia politician, Madison wrote: "The Senate have sent back the plan of amendments with some alterations which strike in my opinion at the most salutary articles." (In this context, "salutary" means "beneficial.") And indeed, the Senate had whittled down the list of amendments passed by the House from seventeen to twelve.

After a House-Senate committee ironed out some differences between the two versions, the twelve amendments were sent to the states for ratification. The states ratified ten of the twelve, omitting the first proposed amendment, which contained a formula to calculate the number of representatives in the House, and the second proposed amendment, which placed limitations on congressional pay raises. The remaining ten became the Bill of Rights. (Interestingly, the amendment about congressional pay raises would be ratified as the Twenty-Seventh Amendment more than two hundred years later, in 1992.)

WASHINGTON, HENRY & PENDLETON GOING TO THE FIRST CONGRESS

A lithograph of George Washington, Patrick Henry, and Edmund Pendleton traveling from Virginia to the First Continental Congress in Philadelphia

The Lost Fourteenth would have protected individuals from their state governments. However, the people in power at the time were most worried about their rights being infringed by the federal government; the states, they thought, would better protect their liberty.

But let's pause here and think about whose liberty we're talking about: white people's. State law at this time allowed Black people to be enslaved—no surer threat to liberty than that. When the Fourteenth Amendment was ratified in 1868, it took aim at the same issue Madison identified—protection from state governments—but it did so in the wake of the Civil War and the end of slavery. Unlike Madison's proposed amendment, the Fourteenth was specifically intended to ensure equality for Black Americans.

Whether it ultimately fulfilled that promise, however, would be a different story.

★ ★ ★ ★ ★ ★ ★ ★ **Chapter 2** ★ ★ ★ ★ ★ ★ ★ ★

The Civil War and the Civil Rights Act of 1866

The Fourteenth Amendment, ratified in the years after the Civil War, sought to ensure equality for Black Americans after slavery's end. Since the 1600s, Black people had been kidnapped from their home countries in Africa and brought against their will to North America. Millions died on the journey, and those who survived were forced into slavery and treated as less than human. White people justified their actions with racist claims that Black people were inferior to them, suggesting that this meant Black people benefited from being enslaved.

At the time of the Declaration of Independence, slavery was legal in all thirteen colonies. Over time, however, that began to change—by the 1850s, slavery was banned in about half the states. The line between "slave" states and "free" states divided the United States across the middle, and it also was tied to political parties: Republicans were more often antislavery, and Democrats were more often proslavery. Although "enslavers came from all parts of the political spectrum," the *Washington Post* reports, "the most common political affiliation among enslavers was the Democratic Party."

A map from the 1850s showing states that banned slavery in red and those that allowed it in blue

By 1860, about 10 percent of Black people in the United States were free, amounting to almost 500,000 people. About half lived in the North, and about half in the South. Even for free Black people, however, "laws were still in place that limited their liberty—in many areas in the North and the South, they could not own firearms, testify in court or read and write."

In the 1857 case of *Dred Scott v. Sandford*, the Supreme Court ruled that Black people, whether free or enslaved, didn't have the same constitutional protections as white people. The *Dred Scott* decision laid the groundwork for the Civil War, the Civil Rights Act of 1866, and—eventually—the Fourteenth Amendment. In this chapter, we'll explore the lead-up to the Fourteenth Amendment, considering along the way what it means to be a citizen, the effects of war, and the role of white supremacy and capitalism.

Frederick Douglass and Citizenship

Frederick Douglass was a Black man who had illegally taught himself to read before escaping from his enslavers. He went on to become a leading activist, author, and orator who traveled the world speaking out against slavery. On July 5, 1852, Douglass delivered his famous speech "What, to the Slave, Is the Fourth of July?" to a group of white antislavery advocates in Rochester, New York. He explained that the Fourth of July was no celebration to him, as he could not enjoy any of the rights of U.S. citizens:

> *I say it with a sad sense of the disparity between us. I am not included within the pale of this glorious anniversary! Your high independence only reveals the immeasurable distance between us. The blessings in which you, this day, rejoice, are not enjoyed in common.—The rich inheritance of justice, liberty, prosperity and independence, bequeathed by your fathers, is shared by you, not by me. The sunlight that brought life and healing to you, has brought stripes and death to me. This Fourth July is yours, not mine. You may rejoice, I must mourn.*

Among abolitionists (people who wanted to abolish slavery), there were three main theories about the Constitution. The first group thought the Constitution's oblique references to slavery meant that the document was "a covenant with Death and an agreement with Hell" and "null and void before God." They proposed dissolving the Constitution or at the very least amending it.

A second group said that the Constitution was "antislavery in spirit," even though it may have had some clauses that acknowledged slavery. This group proposed passing new federal laws to abolish slavery, but not necessarily rewriting the Constitution.

An image of Frederick Douglass from 1856

A third group suggested that slavery was actually already forbidden by the Constitution, and in particular by the Fifth Amendment's due process clause. The due process clause says the government has to follow fair legal procedures before it can take away your "life, liberty, or property," and this group argued that enslaved people had their liberty taken from them without any fair legal procedures. They believed that the Constitution as it was written could be used to help abolish slavery.

The first group thought the third group's argument was very weak. As we saw in chapter 1, the Constitution affirmed and protected the existence of slavery in numerous places—how could you argue that the same document also *forbade* slavery? Still, advocates often choose to argue for creative interpretations of existing laws and constitutional provisions, since it can be easier to convince a court to interpret a law in your preferred way than it is to convince Congress to pass a new law or amend the Constitution.

CHANGE IN THE LAWS VERSUS THE COURTS

When people want to make political change, they may advocate for new laws or constitutional amendments. After mass shootings, for example, people who favor gun control often suggest that new federal gun laws be passed; some even argue that the Constitution be amended to repeal the Second Amendment. These methods are both quite difficult.

Passing a Federal Law

A federal bill can start in either chamber of Congress—the Senate or the House of Representatives. If more than half of the chamber in which it was introduced votes in favor of the bill, it moves on to the other chamber. If the bill then receives more than half of the vote in the second chamber, it moves on to the president's desk. The president can either sign the bill or veto it. If the president signs the bill, it becomes law. If the president vetoes a bill, it won't become law unless Congress overrides the president's veto, which it can do if two-thirds of each chamber votes in favor of the bill.

Amending the Federal Constitution

There are two paths to amending the U.S. Constitution. The first requires two-thirds in both the House and the Senate to vote in favor of the amendment, and then three-fourths of the fifty states—thirty-eight of them—to sign on.

The second path requires holding another Constitutional Convention. Two-thirds of state legislatures would need to call for such a convention, where the new amendment would be proposed. The amendment would then need to be ratified by three-fourths of the states. While it's theoretically possible to change the Constitution this way, it has never actually happened.

Advocates may try to avoid these difficulties by instead arguing in the courts for creative interpretations of existing laws. Unlike passing new laws or amending the Constitution, this method is simpler: It requires persuading only a judge—or, if the case is appealed, a handful of judges. And as we learned earlier, case law (law made by judicial interpretation) has the same effect as legislation (laws passed by Congress or state legislatures).

After carefully studying the Constitution for several years, Frederick Douglass moved from the first group of thinkers to the third. This change happened "gradually and only after much brooding." By 1852, Douglass was arguing publicly that the correct reading of the Constitution was as an antislavery document: "Now, take the constitution according to its plain reading, and I defy the presentation of a single proslavery clause in it. On the other hand it will be found to contain principles and purposes, entirely hostile to the existence of slavery." Douglass wanted to stir up support for the idea that even under the existing Constitution, Black people were citizens.

A few years later, however, the Supreme Court of the United States would issue an opinion saying the opposite.

Dred Scott

To be a citizen of the United States means that you are entitled to certain rights, like voting. (We'll talk more about this later, when we discuss immigration in chapter 9.) In 1857, the Supreme Court ruled that Black people were not citizens of the United States and never could be.

The plaintiff in that case was Dred Scott, an enslaved Black man. Together with his wife, Harriet, Dred Scott filed a petition to sue for his freedom in Missouri state court in 1846. Before moving to Missouri, Scott had spent several years living with his enslaver in the free state of Illinois and free territory of Wisconsin. He argued to the court that because he had once lived in a free state, he was a free citizen, regardless of whether his enslaver intended to free him or not.

At that time, lawsuits like Scott's were relatively common; when he brought his case, about a hundred other enslaved people in Missouri had won their freedom by arguing that they became free when they entered a free state—what was known as the "then well-recognized rule of 'once free, always free.'" This rule had been established by the Missouri Supreme Court in an 1824 case, but by the time Dred Scott's case made it to the Missouri Supreme Court, the court's composition had changed to be majority proslavery. So despite the 1824 case, the Missouri Supreme Court ruled against Scott.

Scott decided to sue again in federal court on a different theory: He argued that his enslaver had physically harmed and wrongfully imprisoned him. His federal case made it all the way to the U.S. Supreme Court, which, like the Missouri Supreme Court, was majority proslavery at the time.

In a now-infamous decision written by Chief Justice Roger Taney, the U.S. Supreme Court ruled 7–2 against Scott. First, the court held that Scott couldn't sue in federal court because he wasn't a citizen of the United States and that Black people—whether free or enslaved—could never be citizens. Taney wrote for the court:

> *In the opinion of the court, the legislation and histories*
> *of the times, and the language used in the Declaration of*
> *Independence, show, that neither the class of persons who had*
> *been imported as slaves, nor their descendants, whether they*

An issue of Frank Leslie's Illustrated Newspaper from 1857, depicting Dred Scott, his wife, and his daughters. The text is hard to make out, but it describes how Scott was pressured against his wishes to "get his portrait" for the paper.

had become free or not, were then acknowledged as a part of
the people, nor intended to be included in the general words
used in that memorable instrument . . .

They [Black people] had for more than a century before
been regarded as beings of an inferior order, and altogether
unfit to associate with the white race, either in social or
political relations; and so far inferior, that they had no rights
which the white man was bound to respect; and that the
negro might justly and lawfully be reduced to slavery for his
benefit. He was bought and sold, and treated as an ordinary
article of merchandise and traffic, whenever a profit could be
made by it. This opinion was at that time fixed and universal
in the civilized portion of the white race.

The Supreme Court used the Declaration of Independence, which had been created by white property owners, to determine that the white framers of the Constitution did not intend to include Black people as U.S. citizens. Repeating the hateful theories that many white people used to justify slavery, the court wrote that Black people were "beings of an inferior order" who benefited from being enslaved. The court went on to explain that if Black people were citizens, they'd be entitled to the same rights white people had, which the court believed should never happen:

It would give to persons of the negro race, who were
recognized as citizens in any one State of the Union, the
right to enter every other State whenever they pleased, singly
or in companies, without pass or passport, and without
obstruction, to sojourn there as long as they pleased, to go
where they pleased at every hour of the day or night without

molestation unless they committed some violation of law
for which a white man would be punished; and it would
give them the full liberty of speech in public and in private
upon all subjects upon which its own citizens might speak;
to hold public meetings upon political affairs, and to keep
and carry arms wherever they went. And all of this would
be done in the face of the subject race of the same color, both
free and slaves, and inevitably producing discontent and
insubordination among them, and endangering the peace
and safety of the State.

In the court's racist view, giving Black people equal rights would endanger "the peace and safety of the State." So it concluded that Black people could never be citizens.

The court also ruled that Congress couldn't ever interfere with slavery's spread. If Congress banned slavery in a particular state, the court said, this would violate the enslaver's right to his property. To the court, Black freedom was less important than the white man's freedom to enslave.

You might be wondering what this Congress issue had to do with the specific question in the case, whether Dred Scott could sue in federal court. The answer is, absolutely nothing. As historian Paul Finkelman explains, the court went beyond the issues that were presented to it in order to "settle the slavery question once and for all."

But the decision had the opposite effect. After it was announced, many Americans were in an uproar. Antislavery Republicans called the judgment "wicked" and "abominable," and white abolitionist John Brown led an armed uprising at Harpers Ferry, Virginia, that terrified many enslavers. Proslavery Democrats started using the term "Black Republicanism" to tie their political opponents to people like John Brown.

More than anything, the Democrats were afraid that Republicans wanted to end slavery. Slavery powered the southern economy; enslaved people were forced to pick the cotton that was then the South's biggest export. "By the eve of the Civil War," professor Matthew Desmond explains, "the Mississippi Valley was home to more millionaires per capita than anywhere else in the United States." To maintain this wealth, the South had to maintain the institution of slavery.

The final straw for the proslavery South was when Abraham Lincoln, a Republican politician who had publicly criticized the *Dred Scott* ruling, won the 1860 election for president.

The Civil War (1861–1865)

After Lincoln won, but before he was sworn in, South Carolina, Mississippi, Florida, Alabama, Georgia, Louisiana, and Texas all seceded from the United States, soon to be followed by Virginia, Arkansas, North Carolina, and Tennessee. These eleven states became known as the Confederacy, and the North became known as the Union.

The South seceded because it thought Lincoln would ban slavery. South Carolina, for example, said it was seceding because of "an increasing hostility on the part of the non-slaveholding States to the institution of slavery," and Mississippi claimed its secession was "thoroughly identified with the institution of slavery— the greatest material interest of the world."

The Civil War between the Union and Confederacy officially began in April 1861, when Confederate soldiers fired at Fort Sumter in Charleston, South Carolina. Lincoln thought the conflict would be over quickly, but it dragged on for years.

While the South seceded to protect slavery—and while the Civil War did ultimately end slavery—that wasn't the Union's goal at first. "The North initially went to war to hold the nation together," sociologist James W. Loewen explains. "Abolition came later." As President Lincoln wrote in 1862:

> *If I could save the Union without freeing any slave, I would do it; and if I could save it by freeing all the slaves, I would do it; and if I could save it by freeing some and leaving others alone, I would also do that. What I do about slavery and the colored race, I do because I believe it helps to save the Union; and what I forbear, I forbear because I do not believe it would help to save the Union.*

President Lincoln argued for the gradual abolition of slavery. He also believed there was "a physical difference between the white and black races that will for ever forbid the two races from living together on terms of social and political equality." His views on race changed during the Civil War, explains Pulitzer Prize–winning historian Eric Foner, but "he never became a principled egalitarian in the manner of abolitionists such as Frederick Douglass"— which is to say, he didn't believe in equality the way people like Douglass did.

At first, Black people were not allowed to fight for the Union. Frederick Douglass pressured Lincoln to change that; Douglass thought that if Black men went to war for the United States, they could never be denied citizenship. Lincoln initially resisted, but he desperately needed more soldiers as the war waged on. For that reason, in January 1863, he issued the Emancipation Proclamation, which freed enslaved people in the Confederacy and allowed them to fight as soldiers for the Union. Notably, the Emancipation Proclamation didn't abolish slavery altogether; the Thirteenth Amendment would later do that.

It would take another two years for the North to conquer the South, ending the Civil War on April 9, 1865. Over the course of the war, hundreds of thousands of lives were lost—census data suggest the number may be as high as 850,000, or about 3 percent of the country's population at the time. As many as three out of every one hundred Americans died.

After the war ended, Union troops continued to occupy the South in order to keep the peace and protect polling sites. As we'll see, their ability to do so was limited, and mobs of white people would continue to terrorize, assault, and murder newly free Black people in the years after the war.

Presidential Reconstruction and the Right to Vote

After the Civil War ended, Lincoln and his fellow Republicans considered questions of how to "reconstruct" the country. This period, known as Reconstruction, would last from 1865 until 1877.

One of the first issues lawmakers considered during Reconstruction was Black suffrage ("suffrage" means the right to vote). Over the course of the war, around two hundred thousand Black people had served for the Union, including two of Frederick Douglass's sons. As the National Convention of Colored Men put it in 1864:

"Are we good enough to use the bullets, and not good enough to use the ballots? . . . Are we citizens when the nation is in peril and aliens when the nation is in safety?"

RECONSTRUCTION (1865–1877)

As we'll learn in this chapter and the next, during Reconstruction, the country began making progress toward equality. The Thirteenth, Fourteenth, and Fifteenth Amendments were passed, which ended slavery, guaranteed equal protection of the laws, and granted Black people the right to vote, respectively. And for the first time in U.S. history, Black people were able to take positions in both state and federal governments.

But this period would also see an explosion in racist violence, with groups like the Ku Klux Klan emerging to terrorize Black people into subservience. Southern states would also pass "Black codes," laws meant to keep Black people powerless.

The era would come to an end in 1877, when Republican Rutherford B. Hayes became president. The election results were in dispute, and Democrats agreed to recognize Hayes as president so long as Republicans gave them something in exchange: withdrawal of federal troops from the South. Once the troops withdrew, there was no more "enforcement of laws protecting freed slaves," and white supremacy more easily flourished.

Two days after the South surrendered, Lincoln gave a speech in which he proposed that Black people who had served as soldiers should be able to vote: "It is also unsatisfactory to some that the elective franchise is not given to the colored man. I would myself prefer that it were now conferred on the very intelligent, and on those who serve our cause as soldiers." (Note that Lincoln didn't

An 1865 photograph of Black soldiers who fought for the Union during the Civil War

say he thought all Black people should vote—just those who had fought in the Civil War or who were "very intelligent." And remember that women couldn't vote at this time, either.)

The idea of Black suffrage infuriated a man named John Wilkes Booth, who was in the audience. "That is the last speech he will ever make," Booth allegedly said. Three days later, on April 14, 1865, Booth assassinated Lincoln.

Lincoln was succeeded by his vice president, Andrew Johnson. Johnson was a hateful, racist man with sympathies for the Confederacy. In 1865 he is reported to have said, "This is a white man's country, and by God, while I am President, it shall be a white man's Government." Despite those views, he also believed that slavery should be abolished—but not because he believed in equality. Johnson came to oppose slavery during the Civil War because he wanted the war to end more quickly and because he wanted to remain in favor with Northern politicians like Lincoln. Johnson also thought that slavery had a negative effect on the lives of *white* people and that it had hurt the economy of his home state, Tennessee.

Johnson's plan for Reconstruction required only three things of the former Confederate states: abolish slavery, pay back war debts, and pledge allegiance to the Union. He specifically did not require that these southern states grant Black people the right to vote.

On December 6, 1865, the Thirteenth Amendment was ratified. The first section of the Thirteenth officially abolished slavery, and the second section said Congress could pass legislation to enforce the amendment:

Section 1. Neither slavery nor involuntary servitude, except as a punishment for crime whereof the party shall have been duly convicted, shall exist within the United States, or any place subject to their jurisdiction.

Section 2. Congress shall have power to enforce this article by appropriate legislation.

The Thirteenth was the first amendment to expand, rather than limit, the powers of the federal government. As Eric Foner explains, the second section of the amendment gave the federal government "seemingly unlimited authority to prevent actions by states, localities, businesses, and private individuals that sought to maintain or restore slavery."

Previously, most people viewed the national government as the main threat to individual liberties, but the Civil War convinced many white northerners that people had to be protected from their state governments, too. Black Americans already knew this all too well.

The Civil Rights Act of 1866

While the Thirteenth Amendment may have ended slavery, it was not enough to ensure freedom for Black people—let alone to grant them all the rights of citizenship. In 1865 and 1866, right after the amendment was ratified, a set of laws known as the Black codes were enacted throughout the South.

The Black codes effectively reestablished slavery by trapping Black people in exploitative labor contracts and placing Black children in mandatory "apprenticeships." The Black codes also prevented Black people from voting or being on a jury. As Louisiana Republican Benjamin F. Flanders put it at the time: The South's "whole thought and time will be given to plans for getting things back as near to slavery as possible."

In response to the Black codes, Congress passed the Civil Rights Act of 1866 under its Thirteenth Amendment enforcement powers.

The act did two main things. First, it defined citizens as "all persons born in the United States." In this way, the act rejected the *Dred Scott* decision and adopted a rule of birthright citizenship that didn't depend on race. If you were born in the United States, whatever your race, you were a citizen.

Second, the Civil Rights Act of 1866 defined the civil rights owed to all citizens, regardless of race:

> *Citizens, of every race and color, without regard to any*
> *previous condition of slavery or involuntary servitude, except*
> *as a punishment for crime whereof the party shall have been*
> *duly convicted, shall have the same right, in every State and*
> *Territory in the United States, to make and enforce contracts,*

to sue, be parties, and give evidence, to inherit, purchase, lease, sell, hold, and convey real and personal property, and to full and equal benefit of all laws and proceedings for the security of person and property, as is enjoyed by white citizens, and shall be subject to like punishment, pains, and penalties, and to none other, any law, statute, ordinance, regulation, or custom, to the contrary notwithstanding.

Basically, the act covered things like holding property and making contracts—rights critical to full citizenship. The intent of the act was to prevent states from enacting Black codes.

After it was passed by Congress, the Civil Rights Act of 1866 was vetoed by President Johnson. Congress overrode the president's veto—the first time Congress had ever done so for a major piece of legislation—and the act became law on April 9, 1866, a year to the day after the official end of the Civil War.

The Civil Rights Act of 1866 was only a first step in establishing racial equality. It left many questions unanswered, like whether Black people were entitled to serve on juries, vote, or hold office. And states were able to get around the 1866 act by enforcing other laws, like vagrancy laws, against only Black people. Vagrancy laws prohibited things like loitering, which means standing around without a purpose; they were vague enough that they could easily be used to discriminate.

Southern states also found a loophole in the Thirteenth Amendment itself. The amendment's first clause says that slavery is allowed as "punishment for crime"—in other words, incarcerated people could be forced to work without pay. This loophole meant that once Democrats were back in power in the South, they redefined more crimes as felonies, and the prison population skyrocketed. While the laws didn't mention race explicitly, they were enforced unfairly; most of the people imprisoned were Black. Even today, this exception in the Thirteenth Amendment allows for the exploitation of prison labor.

Republicans in Congress, though, were already working on a stronger measure. As we learned earlier in this chapter, it's harder to amend the Constitution than to repeal an ordinary law, which is why Republicans' next goal was passing a constitutional amendment that would help ensure Black equality.

Despite the horrifying ruling in their Supreme Court case, Dred Scott and his family ultimately found freedom—but not from the courts or the justice system. Rather, their enslaver's widow had married a Massachusetts politician who was widely known as an ultra abolitionist. The situation embarrassed the politician, who took steps to free the Scott family. Scott's story shows us that evil may be perfectly legal, and that justice often comes not from the courts but from outside of them.

In this chapter we learned about Dred Scott, the Civil War, Reconstruction, and the Civil Rights Act—all of which led up to the Fourteenth Amendment and demonstrate that the amendment was aimed at Black equality. As we'll see, however, its ability to achieve that goal has been limited. Like the Scott family's story, the story of the Fourteenth Amendment shows us the limits of law.

But before we get there, we first must understand the amendment itself.

★ ★ ★ ★ ★ ★ ★   Chapter 3   ★ ★ ★ ★ ★ ★ ★

The Birth of the Fourteenth Amendment

After the Civil War, the Fourteenth Amendment was passed to ensure that newly free Black people would receive equal rights. It was part of a set of what are called the Reconstruction amendments, which also include the Thirteenth Amendment (ending slavery) and the Fifteenth Amendment (allowing Black men to vote). Together, these three amendments would so fundamentally reshape the Constitution that some scholars refer to their ratification as the second founding.

In this chapter, we'll work to better understand the Fourteenth Amendment by diving deep into its various sections—considering issues of federalism, white supremacy, and the meaning of citizenship along the way. We'll also discuss the Republicans who worked to get the amendment passed, the period of Radical Reconstruction they helped usher in, and the relationship between progress and political gain.

Joint Committee on Reconstruction

In December 1865, at the urging of Thaddeus Stevens, a Republican representative from Pennsylvania, a Joint Committee on Reconstruction was appointed to conduct hearings to learn what was going on in the South, and to figure out if and how former Confederate states should be represented in Congress. (A joint committee is a group that includes members from both houses of Congress.) The Joint Committee on Reconstruction included Stevens and other Radical Republicans, but they were balanced out by more moderate Republicans like John Bingham of Ohio, and even three Democrats.

A photograph of Thaddeus Stevens from 1863

Stevens had pushed for the joint committee because he felt President Johnson's plan for Reconstruction was failing, as evidenced by the Black codes and violence that ran rampant in the South. Ultimately, the joint committee spent months debating and drafting what would become the Fourteenth Amendment.

WHO WAS JOHN BINGHAM?

Bingham, left, with his fellow prosecutors for the Lincoln assassination conspiracy trial

John Bingham represented Ohio in the House of Representatives from 1855 to 1862 and 1865 to 1872. He graduated from Franklin College, a racially integrated school in Ohio, though he was not an abolitionist until later in his life. In the first half of his congressional career, Bingham's politics aligned with those of Radical Republican colleagues like Stevens, but after losing his bid for reelection in 1862 he became viewed as a moderate Republican. In 1865, he served as a prosecutor for President Abraham Lincoln's assassination conspiracy trial. During his time on the Joint Committee on Reconstruction, Bingham crafted much of the language at the core of the Fourteenth Amendment.

Much of the Fourteenth Amendment was inspired by antislavery theory and language. Fourteenth Amendment drafters like Stevens and Bingham had worked in antislavery politics for years, and they brought those ideas and phrases with them to the joint committee.

The first issue tackled by the joint committee, though, was voting. The committee had been struggling with an ironic consequence of the Thirteenth Amendment: The South would have more power in Congress now that the Constitution's three-fifths clause was invalid. That clause said that only three-fifths of enslaved people counted toward how many representatives a state got—a cruel and racist provision that dehumanized Black people. Once the Thirteenth Amendment was ratified, all Black people counted for purposes of congressional representation. That meant the South would have two-fifths more representatives than before the war, yet all those representatives would be elected by white people because President Johnson hadn't required that southern states let Black people vote.

The obvious answer should have been to simply give Black people the right to vote, but most congressmen at the time (except for the Radical Republicans) thought that was too liberal. So the joint committee figured out another way to reduce southern representation while still allowing states to prevent Black people from voting. The solution they settled on was to punish states that denied the vote to people based on "race or color" by subtracting those people from the population used to calculate the state's number of representatives. Because the North had a relatively small Black population (less than 2 percent of the total population), this clause would barely affect northern states' congressional representation, even if they refused to let Black people vote.

In January 1866, the first version of the Fourteenth Amendment, which had only the clause about voting, passed the House of Representatives. In the Senate, the amendment was opposed by Radical Republicans, who thought it was too conservative because it did not give Black men the right to vote, and by Democrats, who thought it was too liberal because it punished states that suppressed Black voting. Together with other Black leaders, Frederick Douglass sent a petition to the Senate opposing the amendment, explaining that they "most respectfully but earnestly pray this honorable body to favor no amendment to the Constitution of the United States which will grant or allow any one or all of the States of this Union to disfranchise any class of citizens on the ground of race or color for any consideration whatever." The amendment failed to get the necessary votes to pass the Senate, so it was back to the drawing board for the joint committee.

Throughout the spring of that year, the joint committee kept working on different versions of the Fourteenth Amendment. The committee held numerous hearings on the atrocities happening in the South, learning from witnesses of the attacks against Black people and Union supporters. In the report it eventually produced, the committee wrote:

> The feeling in many portions of the country towards
> emancipated slaves, especially among the uneducated and
> ignorant, is one of vindictive and malicious hatred. This
> deep-seated prejudice against color is assiduously cultivated
> by the public journals, and lends to acts of cruelty, oppression,
> and murder, which the local authorities are at no pains
> to prevent or punish. There is no general disposition to
> place the colored race, constituting at least two-fifths of the
> population, upon terms even of civil equality. While many

instances may be found where large planters and men of the
better class accept the situation, and honestly strive to bring
about a better order of things, by employing the freedmen
at fair wages and treating them kindly, the general feeling
and disposition among all classes are yet totally averse to the
toleration of any class of people friendly to the Union, be
they white or black; and this aversion is not unfrequently
manifested in an insulting and offensive manner.

In April 1866, the committee settled on a five-section draft that combined many desired constitutional changes. The committee hoped that the more popular sections would offset the less popular ones, and everything would get passed at once.

This draft of the Fourteenth Amendment passed both the House and the Senate, where an introductory sentence about birthright citizenship was added. The final version of the Fourteenth Amendment approved by Congress had many parts: the birthright citizenship clause, a privileges or immunities clause, a due process clause, an equal protection clause, a suffrage clause, insurrection clauses, and an enforcement clause. Let's get into it!

Birthright Citizenship Clause (Section 1)

All persons born or naturalized in the United States, and subject to the jurisdiction thereof, are citizens of the United States and of the State wherein they reside.

The Fourteenth Amendment's birthright citizenship clause was a direct response to *Dred Scott*, which said Black people could not be U.S. citizens, and an echo of the Civil Rights Act of 1866, which said anyone born on U.S. soil was a citizen. This clause also made clear that anyone born in the United States was a citizen of both the United States *and* the state where they live, regardless of their race. (The court in *Dred Scott* had created a distinction between state and national citizenship, holding that being a citizen of a state does not necessarily make you a citizen of the United States.) In this way, the amendment created a single citizenship.

Even though the birthright citizenship clause is the first part of the amendment, it was actually a last-minute addition. During the debates, Jacob Howard, a Radical Republican from Michigan on the joint committee, proposed settling "the great question of citizenship" with language explicitly rejecting the logic of *Dred Scott*. While the Civil Rights Act of 1866 had also sought to do so, Congress wanted to make the definition of a citizen harder to change by enshrining it in the Constitution. Keep this in mind for the next chapter, when we learn how the Supreme Court interpreted the language of this clause.

Privileges or Immunities Clause (Section 1)

No State shall make or enforce any law which shall abridge the privileges or immunities of citizens of the United States;

A "privilege" is something you are entitled to, and an "immunity" is something you are protected from. This clause says that states cannot get in the way of the "privileges or immunities" granted to all U.S. citizens.

So what, exactly, are those privileges or immunities? Repeatedly and publicly, John Bingham explained that this clause referred to the rights granted by the first eight amendments in the Bill of Rights. At the time, the Bill of Rights protected people only from actions taken by the *federal* government—the Supreme Court had made this clear in an 1833 case called *Barron v. Baltimore*. The privileges or immunities clause was added to give people those same rights against their *state* governments.

In this way, the privileges or immunities clause had the same goal as James Madison's Lost Fourteenth: to protect citizens from both levels of government. In fact, Bingham's proposal was actually *more* protective than Madison's; where Madison had listed only a few rights, Bingham's covered all "privileges or immunities."

The privileges or immunities clause was necessary because state governments were violating their citizens' rights—particularly the rights of their Black citizens. Constitutional historian Michael Curtis explains that because *Barron v. Baltimore* said that the Bill of Rights didn't apply to state governments, southern states were "free to suppress speech and press on the question of slavery" and "free to deny . . . rights to blacks." And indeed, Black people were being denied the right to a trial by an impartial jury and the right to bear arms, and laws were passed to punish people of all races for speaking out against slavery.

None of this violated the U.S. Constitution because these were state, not federal, laws. Again, the Bill of Rights did not apply to state governments at the time. And while the state laws may have violated some state constitutions, state courts repeatedly failed to block them. Bingham hoped that the privileges or immunities clause would prevent states from depriving their citizens of fundamental rights because those citizens would be able to sue under the U.S. Constitution in federal courts, which he believed were more impartial.

FREE SPEECH AND SLAVERY

Before the Civil War, states across the country were suppressing criticism of slavery by violating the free speech rights of their citizens (both Black and white)—even where their state constitutions protected the right to free speech.

For example, a Virginia law punished any "free person" who "by speaking or writing maintains that owners have no right of property in slaves." An 1853 publication about slavery law catalogs several others, some of which were punishable by death:

- In Louisiana, "if any person shall use any language from the *bar*, *bench*, *stage*, *pulpit*, or in any other place, or hold any conversation having a *tendency* to promote discontent among free colored people, or insubordination among slaves, he may be imprisoned at hard labor not less than three nor more than twenty-one years; or he may suffer death, at the discretion of the court."

- "In Mississippi, a white man, who prints or circulates doctrines, sentiments, advice, or *innuendoes*, likely to produce discontent among the colored class, is fined from one hundred to a thousand dollars, and imprisoned from three to twelve months."

- "For publishing, or circulating, in the state of North Carolina, any pamphlet or paper having an *evident tendency* to excite slaves, or free persons of color, to insurrection or resistance, imprisonment not less than one year, *and* standing in the pillory *and* whipping, at the discretion of the court, for the first offense, and death for the second." In Georgia the same offense was punishable by death, without any reservation. In Louisiana, it was either life imprisonment or death, at the discretion of the court. In Virginia, the first offense got thirty-nine lashes, the second, death.

- In Tennessee, simply receiving an antislavery document in the mail could lead to "an infamous punishment—a penitentiary offense of five years' confinement!"

The suppression of antislavery sentiment wasn't always done with laws. Many southern mail carriers, for example, simply refused to deliver abolitionist literature. And white mobs repeatedly destroyed the press of Reverend Elijah Lovejoy, who published antislavery editorials in his religious newspaper. In 1837, he was murdered by one such mob during an attack on his press in Alton, Illinois.

THE PRO-SLAVERY RIOT OF NOVEMBER 7, 1837. DEATH OF REV. E. P. LOVEJOY.

A woodcut of the mob attacking Reverend Lovejoy

Even though many state constitutions explicitly protected free speech rights, state courts refused to enforce these provisions—and federal courts couldn't hear cases under state constitutions. Back in 1789, James Madison had specifically wanted to protect people against "departures from their own constitutions by state courts, which might be susceptible to local influences or to the special mood or motivation that could cause oppressive actions." And indeed, Madison also worried that the

Bill of Rights didn't protect against "that quarter where the greatest danger lies"—not the government, but people operating as "the majority against the minority."

The suppression of free speech wasn't just limited to state governments. In 1836, the U.S. House of Representatives passed a rule that said its members couldn't take action on petitions or other papers relating to slavery or abolition.

Ultimately, all this backfired. Petitions to Congress skyrocketed after the 1863 rule; Elijah Lovejoy became a martyr; and people who weren't abolitionists nevertheless critiqued mob violence and state restrictions on speech.

Free speech eventually became part of the Republican platform. In 1856, Republican John C. Fremont ran for president with the slogan "Free Speech, Free Press, Free Soil, Free Men, Fre-mont and Victory!" And in 1860, Republicans in Congress voted for an amendment to a resolution that said no state could interfere with free speech and press:

> But free discussion of the morality and expediency of slavery should never be interfered with by the laws of any State, or of the United States; and the freedom of speech and of the press, on this and every other subject of domestic and national policy, should be maintained inviolate in all the States.

That proposal failed, but the same goal would be achieved by the Fourteenth Amendment, which was meant to incorporate free speech as one of the "privileges or immunities" that states couldn't infringe.

The struggle to tell the truth about racism didn't end in the 1800s. Today, numerous states have passed bills banning public schools from teaching critical race theory, a doctrine that explores institutional and systemic racism. Legislators have argued that these laws are necessary because talking about the racism built into the fabric of the United States will "make kids feel bad"—

But why did Bingham use those weird words "privileges or immunities"? Why didn't he just say, hey, the first eight amendments
apply to state governments, too?

Bingham was intentionally vague because he wanted to incorporate more rights than just those eight amendments—like the rights
in various state constitutions and in the Civil Rights Act of 1866.
"By the mid-1870s," writes Eric Foner, "the idea that the Fourteenth
Amendment 'incorporated' the Bill of Rights had become, as far as
Republicans were concerned, a virtually uncontroversial *minimum*
interpretation of the amendment's purposes" (italics added).

INCORPORATION

"Incorporation" is a specialized term that will be used throughout
this book. It refers to the process by which the Bill of Rights
became applicable to state governments. Although Bingham
intended the privileges or immunities clause to incorporate the
Bill of Rights—to make it applicable to state governments—we'll
learn in chapter 6 that incorporation wound up happening in far
more a surprising way.

Opponents worried that the Fourteenth Amendment would be
a "deep and revolutionary" change to state government. But this
was accurate—"deep and revolutionary" change was the point! In
the next chapter, we'll see how the Supreme Court disregarded this
intent in narrowly interpreting the purposes of the privileges or
immunities clause and the Fourteenth Amendment as a whole.

Due Process Clause (Section 1)

. . . nor shall any State deprive any person of life, liberty, or property, without due process of law . . .

The due process clause looks very similar to the Fifth Amendment, which says "no person shall be . . . deprived of life, liberty, or property, without due process of law." Both the Fifth and Fourteenth Amendments say that the government has to give you fair legal procedures before it can take away your life, liberty, or property.

But if the privileges or immunities clause was supposed to make the Bill of Rights (including the Fifth Amendment) applicable to state governments, why was the due process clause even necessary? The answer is in the specific language used by these two clauses: The privileges or immunities clause says it applies only to citizens. But the due process clause says it applies to "any person"—citizen or not. That wasn't an accident; Bingham emphasized that all people were entitled to due process, regardless of their citizenship status. We'll learn more about this in chapter 9, on immigration.

Equal Protection Clause (Section 1)

. . . nor deny to any person within its jurisdiction the equal protection of the laws.

Like the due process clause, the equal protection clause applies to all people, not just citizens. Its intent initially was to protect the rights of Black people after the Civil War—much like the Civil Rights Act of 1866, which said that all citizens were entitled to "full and equal benefit of all laws and proceedings for the security of person and property as is enjoyed by white citizens."

The equal protection clause, however, isn't limited to race—it applies to *any* law that improperly targets certain groups of people. We'll learn more about this in chapter 7, when we discuss what are known as the "tiers of scrutiny."

Suffrage Clause (Section 2)

Representatives shall be apportioned among the several States according to their respective numbers, counting the whole number of persons in each State, excluding Indians not taxed. But when the right to vote at any election for the choice of electors for President and Vice-President of the United States, Representatives in Congress, the Executive and Judicial officers of a State, or the members of the Legislature thereof, is denied to any of the male inhabitants of such State, being twenty-one years of age, and citizens of the United States, or in any way abridged, except for participation in rebellion, or other crime, the basis of representation therein shall be reduced in the proportion which the number of such male citizens shall bear to the whole number of male citizens twenty-one years of age in such State.

Section 2 says that if a state prevents part of its population from voting, the state would lose that proportion of its representation in Congress. In all of U.S. history, Section 2 has never actually been used to punish any behavior, in part because of how difficult it is to determine the percentage of people who were prevented from voting.

Another flaw of this provision, which was explicitly pointed out to the joint committee, is that states could not be punished for enacting voting restrictions that had disproportionate effects on

Black people but were not explicitly based on race. As we'll learn in chapter 7, states would soon pass restrictions like literacy tests and property qualifications that took advantage of this loophole.

Section 2 upset many women's rights advocates because it mentioned only "male" inhabitants. At the time, even most Radical Republicans didn't support women voting. But when white women's rights advocates like Susan B. Anthony and Elizabeth Cady Stanton talked about their opposition to Section 2, they often talked about it in racist terms, arguing that white women were more deserving of the right to vote than Black men. Here, as elsewhere, it's important to recognize how people can have complicated beliefs—like supporting gender but not race equality or supporting race but not gender equality—and to think about how people's identities can influence which beliefs they hold.

Insurrection Clauses (Sections 3 and 4)

SECTION 3. No person shall be a Senator or Representative in Congress, or elector of President and Vice-President, or hold any office, civil or military, under the United States, or under any State, who, having previously taken an oath, as a member of Congress, or as an officer of the United States, or as a member of any State legislature, or as an executive or judicial officer of any State, to support the Constitution of the United States, shall have engaged in insurrection or rebellion against the same, or given aid or comfort to the enemies thereof. But Congress may by a vote of two-thirds of each House, remove such disability.

This clause prevents anyone who has engaged in "insurrection or rebellion" against the United States—former Confederate soldiers, for example—from holding office. The joint committee drafted this provision because the Black codes convinced them that former Confederates wouldn't support racial equality.

Section 3 arose again after the 2021 Capitol riots. In 2023, the Colorado supreme court held that former president Donald Trump should be disqualified from running for office because he "engaged in insurrection." On appeal, the U.S. Supreme Court overruled the Colorado decision, holding that only Congress—not the states—could disqualify a candidate from a federal position.

SECTION 4. The validity of the public debt of the United States, authorized by law, including debts incurred for payment of pensions and bounties for services in suppressing insurrection or rebellion, shall not be questioned. But neither the United States nor any State shall assume or pay any debt or obligation incurred in aid of insurrection or rebellion against the United States, or any claim for the loss or emancipation of any slave; but all such debts, obligations and claims shall be held illegal and void.

In Section 4, the joint committee dealt with war debts by prohibiting the federal government from paying the Confederacy's debts or compensating enslavers for loss of property. This provision doesn't come up much today.

Enforcement Clause (Section 5)

The Congress shall have the power to enforce, by appropriate legislation, the provisions of this article.

The enforcement clause gives Congress the power to pass "appropriate legislation" to "enforce" the Fourteenth Amendment. This wording, law professor Akhil Reed Amar explains, was intended to be "transformative" and "to uproot all vestiges of unfreedom and inequality." The Fourteenth Amendment was meant to continually adapt over time, not to be frozen in the 1800s.

As we'll see in the next chapter, the intent of Section 5 was to let Congress pass laws that targeted private action, like mob violence. The joint committee heard extensive testimony about how private parties were harming and intimidating Black people and Union loyalists. As with many other parts of the Fourteenth Amendment, however, the Supreme Court would interpret this provision narrowly.

Ratification and Radical Reconstruction

Radical Republicans thought the Fourteenth Amendment didn't go far enough because it didn't grant Black men the right to vote. (As Radical Republican Thaddeus Stevens said: "It falls far short of my wishes.") Democrats, on the other hand, thought the Fourteenth Amendment went too far. The amendment felt like a compromise that satisfied nobody.

Nevertheless, in June 1866, the amendment passed Congress and was sent to the states for ratification. Most northern states voted to ratify, but nearly every southern state rejected it. This ultimately convinced moderate Republicans that they needed to find a way to give Black men the right to vote, as they thought Black voters would elect state congressmen who supported the amendment. (It may seem odd today that moderate Republicans would support civil rights but not voting rights for Black people. At the time, however, voting was viewed as a "political privilege granted to a few citizens rather than as a right belonging to all.")

So Republicans in Congress passed the first Reconstruction Act of 1867, which placed former Confederate states under military rule and imposed several requirements: their new governments had to be elected by both white and Black men, they had to adopt new constitutions that said Black people could vote, and they had to ratify the Fourteenth Amendment. This period later became known as Radical Reconstruction.

For the first time in American history, Black men were elected to state legislatures. Once these new biracial governments were elected, seven of the southern states that had originally rejected the amendment changed course, and the Fourteenth Amendment was finally ratified in July 1868. Eric Foner explains the irony: "The framers of the Fourteenth Amendment studiously avoided including black suffrage among its provisions. But without the votes of black men in southern elections and legislatures, the amendment could never have become part of the Constitution." To add to the hypocrisy, the Reconstruction Act of 1867 meant that Black men could vote in the South but not in the rest of the country.

This would soon be addressed by the Fifteenth Amendment, ratified in 1870, which guaranteed that a citizen's right to vote couldn't be denied "on account of race, color, or previous condition of servitude." Together with the Fourteenth, this amendment was meant to guarantee equal rights to people recently freed from slavery (or at least the men).

That same year, Congress passed the Civil Rights Enforcement Act of 1870, which "reenacted" the Civil Rights Act of 1866. The 1870 act clarified that the 1866 act was passed based on Congress's power to enact legislation under both the Thirteenth and Fourteenth Amendments. The 1870 act also targeted mobs, making it a felony for people to conspire to violate someone else's constitutional rights.

By 1870, the country seemed to be making progress. Radical

Reconstruction led to laws against racial discrimination, fairer tax laws, and election of Black people to public office. Sixteen Black people served in Congress during Reconstruction, nine of whom had previously been enslaved. Hundreds of others served as state legislators. By the end of 1870, more than 700,000 Black people registered to vote in southern states.

Earlier that same year, Republican Hiram Revels was elected as the first Black U.S. Senator. Because of his race, some senators had challenged whether he had really been a citizen for the nine years the Constitution required. Neither side convinced the other, but Republicans had more votes, and on February 25, 1870, Hiram Revels took his seat in Congress.

Black congressmen elected during Radical Reconstruction

★ ★ ★

As we saw in this chapter, whether progress is made in achieving equality has a lot to do with who stands to gain politically. Moderate Republicans, for example, agreed to allow Black men to vote only because it would help them pass the Fourteenth Amendment.

Progress is also often short-lived. In 1877, the Reconstruction Era officially ended when Republicans withdrew federal troops from the South in exchange for Democrats recognizing Republican Rutherford B. Hayes as president—a political compromise that would erase the period's gains in racial equality. By 1901, there would no longer be any Black people serving in national office representing the South.

In these same years, as we'll see in part II, the Supreme Court would destroy the core of the Fourteenth Amendment. Bingham thought the "indefiniteness of meaning" of the Fourteenth Amendment—its intentional vagueness—was a "charm" because the amendment could grow and change over time, protecting more people as society changed. But the "indefiniteness of meaning" also meant that courts could interpret the amendment narrowly, and indeed they did—totally disregarding what the Radical Republicans intended the amendment to do.

Part II

THE SUPREME COURT

Limiting the Fourteenth Amendment in Post–Civil War America

So, the Fourteenth Amendment had been ratified. All was well, right?

Wrong. The thing about laws, and constitutional provisions, is that after they're enacted they're interpreted by courts. For example, a person might sue because they think something the government did violates the Constitution. They would bring their case before a court, and the court would say "yes, that's unconstitutional" or "no, it's not." In this way, court opinions (case law) continue to shape what the Constitution means.

In the years after the Fourteenth Amendment was ratified, the Supreme Court would nearly destroy it in a series of cases that limited the amendment's reach. In this chapter, we'll consider several of these cases and the ways they intersect with issues of federalism and white supremacy—issues that continue to arise throughout this book. These cases were decided in the years after the Civil War, when white supremacist groups like the Ku Klux Klan tormented Black people to intimidate them into subservience. Although the Fourteenth Amendment had been passed in response to this mob violence, the Supreme Court repeatedly limited what the Fourteenth Amendment could do to protect Black people.

IDA B. WELLS AND
SOUTHERN HORRORS

Born in 1862, Ida B. Wells was an investigative journalist and civil rights advocate whose writings shed light on the horrific violence white mobs perpetrated against Black people in the years after the Civil War. Her 1892 pamphlet, *Southern Horrors: Lynch Law in All Its Phases*, was written to be "a contribution to truth, an array of facts, the perusal of which it is hoped will stimulate this great American Republic to demand that justice be done."

Ida B. Wells

Wells explained that lynchings were intentionally public events: Mobs of white people brutally murdered Black people in public in order to scare other Black people into subservience. These attacks were rarely investigated by police, and the attackers were almost never sent to prison. The mobs were saying: The law can't protect you; police won't protect you; we are in power.

The white people who committed these lynchings came from all sorts of backgrounds—including, as Wells wrote, "the leading business men, in their leading business centre"—and they tried to make lynchings seem more legitimate by claiming that the Black men they killed had raped white women. Such claims fed off a widespread fear at the time about the "purity" of white women, which supposedly would be spoiled by Black men. Indeed, Wells explained, white men were not punished for having relationships with Black women, "but it is death to the colored man who yields to the force and advances of a similar attraction in white women."

Wells reported that in a period of eight years, 728 Black people were lynched, many of whom were accused of raping white women. Only about a third of those 728 victims had been charged with rape, and many of those charged were almost certainly innocent. One woman's confession illustrated the reasons for such false accusations: "The neighbors saw the fellow here . . . I feared I might give birth to a Negro baby. I hoped to save my reputation by telling you a deliberate lie."

Wells explained that the mobs cared only when white women were raped: "When the victim is a colored woman it is different." These mobs of white people were not actually interested in protecting women from rape; they were interested in perpetuating false accusations of rape against Black men to attempt to legitimize their murders.

Limiting the Privileges or Immunities Clause

The Fourteenth Amendment was ratified in 1868 to ensure equality for Black Americans. By making the Bill of Rights applicable to state governments, for example, the privileges or immunities clause was intended to protect people's fundamental rights regardless of where they lived. This was especially important to Black people, whose rights were often infringed by their state governments. But just five years after the amendment was ratified, in the *Slaughterhouse Cases*, the Supreme Court severely weakened the Fourteenth Amendment by redefining the privileges or immunities clause altogether.

Oddly, the *Slaughterhouse Cases* didn't concern race at all—instead, they were about butchers and livestock. In 1869, Louisiana passed a law that gave Crescent City Livestock Landing and Slaughterhouse Company a monopoly over slaughterhouses in and near New Orleans. (A "monopoly" means to have exclusive control over a trade or industry in a given region.) The 1869 law said that if independent butchers wanted to continue to slaughter animals, they could do so only on Crescent City's grounds, where they would have to pay a fee. The state justified the law by saying it protected public health: The Crescent City slaughterhouse was located downstream of New Orleans, which meant all the animals' blood and guts wouldn't flow into the city's water supply.

The 1869 law raised costs for the independent butchers, who sued over their lost profits. Among other things, the butchers claimed that the state had violated the privileges or immunities clause of the Fourteenth Amendment. They argued that the right to pursue their livelihood as butchers was one of the privileges that the amendment protected.

The Supreme Court ruled against the butchers. In a 5–4 decision, the court said that there were two types of "privileges or immunities"—one state, one federal—and the Fourteenth applied only to the federal ones. Federal privileges included a very limited number of things—like going to Washington to petition the federal government to address grievances and having protection on the high seas—but they did *not* include the right to butcher cattle wherever you like. For that reason, the butchers' Fourteenth Amendment claim failed.

To reach this conclusion, the court focused on certain phrasing in the amendment: "All persons born or naturalized in the United States, and subject to the jurisdiction thereof, are citizens *of the United States and of the State* wherein they reside. No State shall make or enforce any law which shall abridge the privileges or immunities of citizens *of the United States*" (italics added). Considering this language, the court wrote:

> *The language is, "No State shall make or enforce any law which shall abridge the privileges or immunities of citizens* of the United States." *It is a little remarkable, if this clause was intended as a protection to the citizen of a State against the legislative power of his own State, that the word citizen of the State should be left out when it is so carefully used, and used in contradistinction to citizens of the United States, in the very sentence which precedes it. It is too clear for argument that the change in phraseology was adopted understandingly and, with a purpose.*

Based on the text alone, the court distinguished between rights that belonged to citizens of the United States and those that belonged to citizens of a state. The court did not acknowledge that the first clause, about birthright citizenship, had been drafted later and separately (as we learned in chapter 3).

In this way, the court ignored what legislators like John Bingham had intended the amendment to do. Remember, Bingham made clear that the privileges or immunities clause was meant to include all the rights listed in the first eight amendments. As we discussed in the prior chapter, Bingham thought the privileges or immunities clause would "incorporate" the Bill of Rights against state governments (that is, make it applicable to them).

But the Supreme Court was not as radical as Bingham. In the *Slaughterhouse Cases,* the court redefined the privileges or immunities clause to prevent the Bill of Rights from applying to state governments. By doing so, the court undermined and drastically limited the Fourteenth's ability to protect the rights of Black people.

THE SUPREME COURT DOUBLES DOWN

In the years after the *Slaughterhouse Cases* ruling, the Supreme Court repeatedly reaffirmed that the privileges or immunities clause did not incorporate the Bill of Rights against state governments.

In 1875, for example, the Supreme Court decided *Walker v. Sauvinet.* The plaintiff in that case, Joseph Walker, was a white coffeehouse owner who refused to serve a Black man named Charles Sauvinet. At the time, Louisiana had a law that said owners of public places couldn't discriminate against patrons on the basis of race, so Sauvinet brought suit. Sauvinet won, but the trial had no jury.

Walker appealed all the way to the U.S. Supreme Court on the theory that his Sixth Amendment right to trial by jury had been violated. He argued that the Sixth Amendment applied to the actions of state governments because of the privileges or immunities clause in the Fourteenth. The court ruled against him, explaining that the privileges or immunities clause protected only a small number of federal rights. Even though this case was decided in favor of Sauvinet, who was Black, it reaffirmed an understanding of the Fourteenth that was harmful to Black people more generally.

The court reached a similar conclusion two decades later in *O'Neil v. Vermont*. John O'Neil sold liquor in New York, where it was legal, but he also shipped some to Vermont, where it wasn't. He was ultimately sentenced to fifty-five years in prison for his actions, which he argued was cruel and unusual punishment under the Eighth Amendment. Like Joseph Walker, John O'Neil argued that this amendment should be made applicable to state governments under the privileges or immunities clause. But once again, the Supreme Court reaffirmed the *Slaughterhouse Cases* and rejected O'Neil's argument for incorporation.

Limiting the Fourteenth to Government Action

In the *Slaughterhouse Cases*, the Supreme Court limited the Fourteenth Amendment by saying that it did not incorporate the Bill of Rights against state governments. In the years that followed, the court would also make clear that the Fourteenth Amendment could not be used to protect Black people from discrimination by private parties.

Congress passed the Civil Rights Act of 1875—which, among other things, banned segregation in hotels, transportation, theaters, "and other places of public amusement"—to help the Fourteenth Amendment achieve its goal of racial equality. Section 5 of the amendment, known as the enforcement clause, says, "Congress shall have power to enforce, by appropriate legislation, the provisions of this article." The Civil Rights Act of 1875 was the "appropriate legislation" that Congress hoped would help enforce the Fourteenth Amendment.

But the Supreme Court would overturn the 1875 law in the

Civil Rights Cases of 1883. In the *Civil Rights Cases*, the court held that when Congress passes laws under the Fourteenth Amendment's enforcement clause, it can regulate only government and not private action. Private action doesn't mean something sneaky or secret—it refers to things that individual people or companies do. A law regulating government action would be something like "State officials may not refuse to hire an applicant for a government job because of race." A law regulating private action would be something like "No employer can refuse to hire a job applicant because of race."

Because the Civil Rights Act of 1875 banned segregation in private businesses, it regulated private action. In striking down the 1875 law, the Supreme Court explained that the Fourteenth Amendment "does not authorize Congress to create a code of municipal law for the regulation of private rights; but to provide modes of redress against the operation of State laws, and the actions of State officers." Protecting Black people from discrimination by private parties, however, was part of what the Fourteenth Amendment was intended to address; "equal protection of the laws" was really supposed to mean protection. To add insult to injury, the Supreme Court wrote that Black people no longer needed "to be the special favorite of the laws"—just twenty years after slavery had ended.

A few years before the *Civil Rights Cases* ruling, the Supreme Court had held unconstitutional a Louisiana equality law that prohibited businesses from discriminating on the basis of race. In *Hall v. DeCuir*, the court said that the law burdened what is known as "interstate commerce" (trade or business between states) in violation of the Constitution. In the court's view, it would be nearly impossible for a business like a rail company to operate in a state like

Louisiana that prohibited segregation as well as a state that *required* segregation, as many did. The people on the train car couldn't immediately segregate or desegregate themselves the second the train crossed state lines. If an antidiscrimination law were to exist, the court concluded, it would have to apply to all states—which meant it would have to be federal.

Together, *Hall* and the *Civil Rights Cases* spelled out a catch-22 for racial equality: *Hall* said that antidiscrimination laws had to be federal, but *Civil Rights Cases* said the federal government couldn't pass antidiscrimination laws under the Fourteenth Amendment if they regulated private behavior. It was as if the Supreme Court did not want there to be any antidiscrimination laws at all.

In these cases, the Supreme Court took what the Radical Republicans had worked so hard for and hollowed it out, despite the drafters' intentions for how the Fourteenth Amendment was meant to be interpreted. What was left was a shell of an amendment: Congress couldn't pass laws to control racial discrimination by private parties, nor were people protected against infringements of the Bill of Rights by state governments. What power did the Fourteenth Amendment have left?

Over time, however, the reach of the Fourteenth Amendment grew. But not in the ways you might expect. At the tail end of the 1800s, the Supreme Court began expanding Fourteenth Amendment rights for corporations, while simultaneously contracting those rights for people accused of crimes. By the end of the century, the court's interpretation of the amendment was miles away from Bingham's intentions.

The Gilded Age and the Due Process Accordion

An accordion is an instrument you can expand and contract to make music, usually while pressing buttons or keys. In the last few decades of the 1800s, known as the Gilded Age, the due process clause of the Fourteenth Amendment grew and shrank like an accordion—but it did so in two very different ways. For employers, the accordion expanded as the Fourteenth Amendment came to protect their ability to exploit workers. For people accused of crimes, the accordion contracted as their rights to a fair trial dwindled. In this chapter, we'll consider these widely differing interpretations of the same clause and the ways capitalism affected the Supreme Court's interpretation of the Fourteenth Amendment.

A painting from the 1890s of a woman playing an accordion

Expanding Due Process for Property

Advancements in industry and technology during the Gilded Age led to an increase in the concentration of individual wealth for a small group of Americans. Some people, referred to as "robber barons," got rich by way of troubling business and labor practices. In response, states passed laws intended to protect workers from employers like railroads and banks. The employers then turned to the courts for protection, arguing that laws that cut into their profits violated the due process clause.

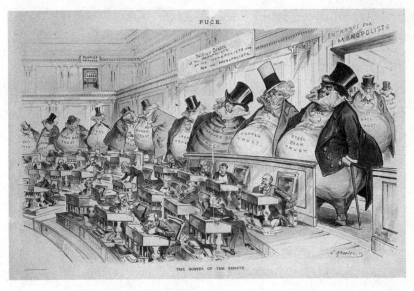

A political cartoon entitled "The Bosses of the Senate" by Joseph Keppler. In this image, business interests, like oil and sugar, are depicted as much larger than the senators, suggesting that these industries were dictating politics. The "peoples' entrance," in the upper left of the image, has a "closed" sign on it.

The employers' argument was not new—the butchers in the *Slaughterhouse Cases* had also tried to make it. In chapter 4, we learned that the butchers argued that the right to butcher cattle wherever they pleased was one of the "privileges or immunities" protected by the Fourteenth Amendment, and that the Supreme Court rejected that argument. But the butchers had also made a different argument: that the law in question violated the due process clause of the Fourteenth Amendment.

If you remember, the due process clause reads, "nor shall any State deprive any person of life, liberty, or property, without due process of law." This means that if the government takes away your life, liberty, or property, it has to provide you with fair proceedings first. The butchers were arguing that because their state, Louisiana, had increased the cost of doing business, they were deprived of property protected by the due process clause.

The Supreme Court disagreed: "Under no construction of that provision that we have ever seen, or any that we deem admissible, can the restraint imposed by the State of Louisiana upon the exercise of their trade by the butchers of New Orleans be held to be a deprivation of property within the meaning of that provision." The court said, in essence, that a slight increase in the cost of doing business didn't count as being deprived of one's property without due process of law. The butchers were still able to practice their profession, even if it cost a little bit more.

In the years that followed, employers kept arguing in court that a loss of profits was a loss of "property"—and they kept losing. Time and again, the Supreme Court would explain that it had already decided the issue, and the due process clause was not applicable to this sort of situation.

Over time, however, the Supreme Court justices who decided the *Slaughterhouse Cases* passed away and were replaced by new justices with new sets of interests and biases. Historian Eric Foner explains that most of the men on the Supreme Court between 1870 and 1900 were "mediocrities . . . from privileged backgrounds" who "had made livings representing railroads and other corporations before joining the court." As the justices changed, so too did the meaning of the due process clause.

"The pressure of the growth of a capital-based system of economic relations," explains civil rights scholar Howard N. Meyer, "and the persuasiveness of the advocates retained by the owners of capital, resulted in the transformation of these words and the reading of an entirely new meaning into them." In other words, the robber barons were able to use their power and money to influence the court's interpretation of the due process clause.

The most important of these cases, *Lochner v. New York*, came in 1905. In order to fight against exploitative labor practices, New York state had passed a law that said bakery employees could work no more than sixty hours a week and no more than ten hours a day. Bakery owner Joseph Lochner was convicted under the law because an inspector found that one of Lochner's employees worked more than sixty hours in a week. After he was found guilty, Lochner appealed to his state appellate courts, which ruled against him. Eventually, his case made it up to the U.S. Supreme Court.

To the surprise of many, the Supreme Court ruled in Lochner's favor. The court overturned the New York law, holding that it violated the due process clause of the Fourteenth Amendment. (Remember, the due process clause reads: "nor shall any State deprive any person of life, *liberty*, or property, without due process of law" [italics added].) Rather than focus on the "property" part of the due process clause, as many prior cases had, the court focused on "liberty."

"Liberty" means freedom, or the ability to do what you please. The right to make contracts, the court explained, was one of the liberties the clause protected. The court held that by preventing people from entering into labor contracts for more than sixty hours per week, the New York law violated its inhabitants' freedom to make contracts.

In reaching this conclusion, the court ignored the power difference between employers and employees—the sixty-hour law at issue was meant to protect workers who might feel like they couldn't say no to a boss's constant requests to work overtime. "What *Lochner* and its successors actually enshrined," explains political science professor Judith A. Baer, "was not the worker's right of contract with respect to hours and conditions of labor, but the employer's right to exploit the employee without state interference."

After *Lochner*, the Supreme Court struck down other laws that were meant to protect workers, like laws that set minimum wages or that regulated child labor. The due process clause was growing, but only for employers.

Limiting Due Process for People

Meanwhile, the due process clause was shrinking for defendants in criminal cases. In *Hurtado v. California* in 1884, the Supreme Court heard the appeal of Joseph Hurtado, who had been convicted of murder in California and sentenced to death. Hurtado argued that because his case hadn't been heard by a grand jury, he had been deprived of his due process right to liberty. "Liberty," here, meant Hurtado's freedom; he lost it when he was put in prison. As we've discussed, the due process clause says that if the government takes your life, liberty, or property, it has to provide you with fair proceedings. Hurtado's claim was that a grand jury was necessary for the proceedings to be fair.

THE GRAND JURY

As explained in chapter 1, a grand jury is a group of people who look at the evidence against you and decide whether you should be brought to trial for a crime. It's different from a regular jury because the grand jury hears evidence presented by only one side, the government's prosecutors.

The idea behind the grand jury is to protect people from false accusations of serious crimes—people shouldn't have to go to trial if there isn't enough evidence. Even if you are ultimately found not guilty, being accused of a crime and having a public trial can have a negative effect on your reputation, job prospects, and relationships. The purpose of a grand jury, whose proceedings are secret, is to protect people from those harms.

The Supreme Court ruled against Hurtado, explaining that a trial could still be fair even without a grand jury—so Hurtado's constitutional rights had not been violated. The court's ruling meant that Hurtado would have to face his death sentence. It also meant that states were free to abolish grand juries if they so chose.

In 1900, the Supreme Court reached a similar conclusion in *Maxwell v. Dow*. Charles Maxwell had been convicted of robbery, but his case hadn't been heard by a grand jury, and his regular jury had only eight members as opposed to the usual twelve. Like Hurtado, Maxwell argued that this violated the Fourteenth Amendment's due process clause by depriving him of his liberty without fair trial proceedings. And like Hurtado, Maxwell failed. The Supreme Court built off its decision in *Hurtado* to hold that the trial could still be fair even if the jury didn't have twelve people on it. The due process clause, therefore, had not been violated.

*The Supreme Court in 1894. Seated, from left: Justices Horace Gray and
Stephen J. Field, Chief Justice Melville W. Fuller, and Justices John Marshall
Harlan and David J. Brewer. Standing, from left: Justices Howell E. Jackson,
Henry B. Brown, George Shiras Jr., and Edward Douglass White.*

Fifteen years later, in 1915, the Supreme Court further limited
the rights of people accused of crimes in *Frank v. Mangum*. Leo
Frank was a northerner who ran a pencil factory in Atlanta, Georgia; he was also Jewish, which made him a minority in Georgia and
a target for antisemitism. Without any definite evidence, Frank
had been charged with a murder.

Public opinion was against him. During Frank's trial, the mob
outside the courthouse was so loud the judge could barely hear the
jury. The hostility concerned the judge so much that just before he
sent the jury out to deliberate, he told the police chief in front of
jurors that he feared a finding of innocence would lead to violence.
When the jury returned, they issued their verdict: Frank was guilty.

Frank appealed to the Georgia Supreme Court, which ruled

against him, and then to the U.S. Supreme Court. He argued that his due process rights had been violated because the threat of mob violence had prevented him from having a fair trial, and that his trial instead had been an "empty form."

A photograph of the Leo Frank trial; Frank is in the center, looking at the camera.

The U.S. Supreme Court agreed that Frank's "allegation that mob domination existed in the trial court might, standing alone and if taken as true, show a condition inconsistent with due process of law"—which is to say, if the court believed Frank, this might be a violation of due process. But rather than look at the facts of Frank's case, the Supreme Court agreed to follow the Georgia Supreme Court's analysis of the mob activity in the trial court, explaining that there was no "reason to suppose that [the Georgia court] did not fairly and justly perform its duty." Because the Georgia Supreme Court ruled against Frank, the U.S. Supreme Court did, too.

But the mob activity all happened at the trial court, not the

Georgia Supreme Court. The U.S. Supreme Court was just as well equipped to review the facts about the violence and intimidation faced by the jurors. It just chose not to.

A photograph of Leo Frank

Not long after the Supreme Court's ruling, the governor of Georgia reduced Frank's sentence from death to life in prison, believing, at least to some degree, in his innocence. Angered by this, a mob broke into the prison where Frank was being held, kidnapped him, and tortured him to death. This tragic end to Frank's life emphasized the point he had tried to make to the Supreme Court: that the mob outside the courthouse would likely have resorted to violence if the jury had found him innocent.

In all these cases, the court narrowed the meaning of the due process clause for defendants in criminal cases. No matter how unfair the trial, nothing seemed to violate the Fourteenth Amendment.

At the turn of the century, the court repeatedly ruled in ways that protected corporate interests and harmed people accused of crimes. These rulings make sense when we consider the court's composition: The justices were sympathetic to the types of corporate interests they had previously represented, and they came from privileged backgrounds, which made it less likely that they would ever face criminal charges like Joseph Hurtado or Leo Frank had.

Soon, however, the Supreme Court would reverse course on both *Frank v. Mangum* and *Lochner v. New York*, as World War I and shifting political tides would convince the court to change its ways.

The Supreme Court Begins to Restore Rights After World War I

From 1914 to 1918, World War I raged in Europe, with the Allies of Great Britain, France, and Russia fighting against the Central Powers of Germany, the Austro-Hungarian Empire, and the Ottoman Empire.

The United States tried to stay out of the war at first, but after the Germans sank several U.S. ships, President Woodrow Wilson felt compelled to enter on the side of the Allies in April 1917. Almost three million men were eventually drafted by the U.S. government to fight in the war.

After World War I, the course of the Supreme Court's opinions started to change. Not only did the court begin to expand due process rights for defendants in criminal cases, but it also began to question laws passed during wartime that stifled free speech. The federal Sedition Act of 1918, for example, made it a crime to "willfully utter, print, write, or publish any disloyal, profane, scurrilous, or abusive language about the form of government . . . or the military or naval forces of the United States." Cases challenging similar state laws ultimately led the Supreme Court to make the Bill of Rights applicable against state governments.

A composite photograph taken by Australian Frank Hurley during World War I, showing the aftermath of a 1917 battle

As we learn about the Supreme Court's rulings in the wake of World War I, several themes from earlier in this book will reemerge, including federalism, white supremacy, and the effects of war. In particular, consider how progress in this chapter was made not for progress's sake, but instead as a reflection of shifting political tides.

Expanding Due Process Rights

In 1919, white planters and merchants in Phillips County, Arkansas (near the town of Elaine) spread the lie that a group of Black people were planning a massacre. In reality, Black sharecroppers had joined a union called the Progressive Farmers and Household Union of America. More than a hundred sharecroppers had gathered for an organizing meeting when several white people fired shots at them. The Black sharecroppers shot back, and a white attacker was killed. In response, armed white mobs murdered more than a hundred Black people over the next few days. This event became known as the Elaine Massacre.

The white people were not prosecuted; the Black sharecroppers were. And much like Leo Frank's trial, jurors faced the threat of mob violence if they found the sharecroppers not guilty. "The Court and neighborhood were thronged with an adverse crowd that threatened the most dangerous consequences to anyone interfering with the desired result," the Supreme Court later wrote about the trial. "There never was a chance for the petitioners to be acquitted; no juryman could have voted for an acquittal and continued to live in Phillips County and if any prisoner by any chance had been acquitted by a jury he could not have escaped the mob." Ultimately, sharecropper Frank Moore and eleven others were convicted of murder and sentenced to death.

The twelve men convicted of murder after the Elaine massacre

The case, *Moore v. Dempsey*, eventually made it to the Supreme Court. Lawyers for the sharecroppers included Moorfield Storey, a white man who was then the president of the National Association for the Advancement of Colored People (NAACP); Ulysses S. Bratton, a white Arkansas attorney; and Scipio A. Jones, a prominent Black attorney and businessman in Arkansas.

Moorfield Storey and Scipio Jones

Despite its similarities to the *Frank v. Mangum* case, which had been decided less than a decade prior, the outcome in *Moore v. Dempsey* was very different. In the intervening years, several justices had left the court, replaced by new justices with new perspectives. As one of the justices who decided *Moore* explained, "Well—Pitney was gone, the late chief was gone, Day was gone—the Court had changed."

But this explanation doesn't account for the fact that two of the justices who ruled against Frank ruled in favor of Moore. Why might their minds have changed?

Scholars suggest it may have been Bratton's excellent oratory—that he painted a vivid picture for the justices about the conditions in the South—or the "the flux in social consciousness" in the time between *Frank v. Mangum* and *Moore v. Dempsey*. During those eight years, World War I had put a spotlight on the United States that may have made the court more sensitive to the world's opinion. The United States had fought for democracy abroad, but cases like *Frank v. Mangum* suggested there was no justice at home.

Whatever the reason, the Supreme Court ruled in favor of Moore, explaining that if the "whole proceeding is a mask," there is no due process. The due process clause was finally being interpreted to protect the rights of people accused of crimes—not just corporate interests.

Several years later, the Supreme Court again ruled that the due process clause protected defendants in criminal cases, in *Powell v. Alabama*, commonly referred to at the time as the "Scottsboro Boys" case. That case was again based on false accusations against Black people, this time nine Black young men from Scottsboro, Alabama, who were traveling on a freight train. A group of white youth had picked a fight with them, and later, two young white women who had been traveling in the same car claimed that the Black teenagers had raped them. While a doctor who examined the two young women said there was no evidence to support their accusations, these facts didn't come out until thirty years later. (As we explored in chapter 4, false accusations of rape by white women were often used to attempt to justify lynchings of Black men.)

Because the teenagers were subject to the death penalty, Alabama was legally required to provide them with lawyers. But no lawyers came forward until the morning of the trial—leaving little time for the attorneys to speak to their clients, let alone pre-

Eight of the nine defendants in the Scottsboro case, along with three NAACP representatives

pare their case. One of the lawyers worked in real estate in another state; the other had no recent experience before a jury. Despite "ample evidence that they were innocent," the nine young men were convicted, and all but the youngest, a thirteen-year-old, were sentenced to death.

On appeal, the Supreme Court considered whether the due process clause protected the defendants: Was "the failure of the trial court to give them reasonable time and opportunity to secure counsel" a "clear denial of due process"?

The eyes of the world were on the U.S. Supreme Court. After the Scottsboro court sentenced the teenagers to death, hundreds of newspaper and magazine articles were published on the case, and activists went on international speaking tours describing the young men's plight. International public opinion may have influenced the court, which ultimately came out in favor of the falsely accused. The Supreme Court held that the due process clause required that a defendant must have an adequate lawyer if the death penalty was at stake. Like *Moore v. Dempsey*, this case broadened the meaning of the due process clause as it applied to defendants in criminal cases.

Around the same time, the Supreme Court also reversed course on its decision in *Lochner*, which had expanded the meaning of the due process clause for employers. As we learned in chapter 5, the *Lochner* case struck down a New York law that limited the number of hours bakery employees could work. The court explained that Mr. Lochner's "liberty" had been violated because he couldn't enter into the sorts of contracts he wanted to enter into.

The *Lochner* era finally ended in 1937 in the case of *West Coast Hotel Co. v. Parrish*. In *West Coast Hotel*, the Supreme Court upheld the constitutionality of a state minimum wage law, allowing plaintiff Elsie Parrish to sue for the difference between what her employer actually paid her and the state's minimum wage. The court effectively overruled *Lochner*, saying that laws restricting the "liberty of contract" were okay if they protected community, health, safety, or vulnerable groups.

What had changed in the years since *Lochner*? This time it was not the eyes of the world, but the eyes of President Franklin Delano Roosevelt. Some scholars suggest that the Supreme Court overruled *Lochner* because President Roosevelt had been planning to "pack the court" by expanding it to fifteen seats (rather than the usual nine) and filling those extra six with more liberal justices. If he did so, the existing conservative justices would no longer be in the majority. The justices wanted to avoid that outcome, so they ruled in a "liberal" way by upholding the minimum wage law at issue in

West Coast Hotel. And indeed, President Roosevelt decided against packing the court—giving this case the nickname "the switch in time that saved nine."

Incorporation of the Bill of Rights

After World War I, the Supreme Court finally began "incorporating" the Bill of Rights, which just means that it started applying the protections in the Bill of Rights to state governments. To put that more concretely, before World War I, you could sue under the First Amendment only if the *federal* government had violated your right to free speech. After the First Amendment was "incorporated," your free speech rights were protected from infringement by your state government, too.

Incorporation wasn't done via the privileges or immunities clause, as John Bingham had anticipated, but instead via the due process clause. (Remember, Bingham thought the "privileges or immunities" that states couldn't infringe were those in the first eight amendments.) Because this is a less obvious way to make the Bill of Rights applicable to state governments, some consider the due process clause a back door to incorporation.

The first few cases that laid the groundwork for First Amendment incorporation seemed like extensions of *Lochner*, in which due process rights were expanded for employers. In *Meyer v. Nebraska*, for example, Robert T. Meyer was convicted for teaching German under a Nebraska law that made it a crime to "teach any subject to any person in any language other than the English language." The Nebraska law had been passed shortly after World War I, when Americans' hostility toward immigrants, and particularly German immigrants, was growing.

The Supreme Court ruled in Meyer's favor, holding that his right to teach and parents' right to hire him were liberties protected by the due process clause. (Again, "liberty" just means the freedom to do as you please.) In *Meyer* and other cases like it, the Supreme Court was twisting itself into knots with its confusing "liberty of contract" language. The court really just wanted to say that the Bill of Rights (and specifically the First Amendment) applied to state governments, which should have been obvious from the privileges or immunities clause. But as civil rights scholar Howard N. Meyer explains:

> *The "privileges" and "immunities" had been erased from the amendment by the tortured reasoning used in the slaughterhouse case and by half a century of bad law built into constitutional practice based on that reasoning, Hurtado had hanged . . . because of it, and the error was too enormous to correct all at once.*

Meyer argues that the Supreme Court was embarrassed about the errors it had made in past cases, when it said that the privileges or immunities clause did not incorporate the Bill of Rights against state governments. Rather than admit its mistakes, the court was looking for other ways to reach the same outcome.

In *Gilbert v. Minnesota*, Justice Louis Brandeis—the first Jewish person on the court—suggested a way for the Supreme Court to save face and start making the Bill of Rights applicable to state governments without reversing a bunch of prior cases. Joseph Gilbert, an organizer for the Nonpartisan League (a farmers' alliance), had been sent to jail because he violated Minnesota law when he spoke negatively about U.S. involvement in World War I. (As we discussed before, state gag laws that stifled freedom of speech were common during World War I.)

The Supreme Court upheld Gilbert's conviction, but Justice Brandeis dissented, saying the Minnesota law deprived Gilbert of his liberty under the U.S. Constitution. He wrote: "I cannot believe that the liberty guaranteed under the Fourteenth Amendment includes only liberty to acquire and to enjoy property." Instead, he suggested that "liberty" might include the free speech rights protected by the First Amendment as well. Even though this was not the majority opinion, Justice Brandeis's dissent laid the groundwork for the incorporation of the Bill of Rights via the due process clause, *not* the privileges or immunities clause.

Brandeis's argument would take center stage in 1925's *Gitlow v. New York*. New York had prosecuted Benjamin Gitlow for criminal anarchy, and while the Supreme Court upheld that conviction, it nevertheless incorporated the First Amendment protections for freedom of speech against state governments via the due process clause. The court said:

> *We may and do assume that freedom of speech and of the press—which are protected by the First Amendment from abridgment by Congress—are among the fundamental personal rights and "liberties" protected by the due process clause of the Fourteenth Amendment from impairment by the States.*

In this way, the due process clause became the back door by which the Bill of Rights was incorporated.

It would take some time, however, before the amendments that related to criminal trials would also be incorporated against state governments. In 1961's *Mapp v. Ohio*, Fourth Amendment protections against improper searches were incorporated via the due process clause, and in 1963's *Gideon v. Wainwright*, the Supreme Court said state courts are required by the Fourteenth Amendment to provide counsel to defendants in criminal cases who can't afford one—thus incorporating the Sixth Amendment's similar federal guarantees. Today, almost all the rights in the Bill of Rights have been incorporated against the states, including most recently in the 2019 case of *Timbs v. Indiana*, which held that the Eighth Amendment prohibition of excessive fines also applied to state governments.

We now have an understanding of what the Fourteenth Amendment says, the context in which it was passed, how the Supreme Court tried to eviscerate it in the years after its ratification, and how the Supreme Court began to restore some of those rights after World War I. In particular, this chapter shows us the impacts of a world war on national politics. It also shows us that progress is often made for political reasons—whether it was international outcry over the Scottsboro case or the court's "switch in time that saved nine."

In Part III, we'll take a look at four areas in which people have used the Fourteenth to fight for equality: race discrimination (chapter 7), gender equality (chapter 8), immigrants' rights (chapter 9), and LGBTQ+ rights (chapter 10). Of course, none of these chapters tell the full story of race, gender, immigration, or LGBTQ+ rights in the United States; they tell the story of where those fights intersect with the Fourteenth Amendment. In each of these areas, the Fourteenth Amendment may have been a starting point, but it isn't the full solution.

Part III

THE PEOPLE

The Fight to End Racial Discrimination

The Reconstruction era ended in 1877, when Republicans made a deal for the presidency. The presidential election results were in dispute, but Democrats agreed to recognize Republican Rutherford B. Hayes as president so long as federal troops were withdrawn from the South.

Once the troops were pulled, former Confederate states sought to reestablish the conditions of slavery. They passed Black codes, which we discussed in chapter 2, and Jim Crow laws, which prohibited Black people from using the same facilities or occupying the same spaces as white people. A 1922 advertisement for St. Luke's Hospital in Richmond, Virginia, for example, proudly proclaimed "no . . . colored patients received." And in Louisiana, a state law required that Black people ride in different train cars from white people.

You might be thinking: Didn't this Louisiana law—which treated Black people differently from white people—violate the Fourteenth Amendment? In an 1896 case called *Plessy v. Ferguson*, the Supreme Court said no.

Although the Fourteenth Amendment was enacted with the

St. Luke's Hospital

Owned and personally conducted by Dr. Stuart McGuire for the exclusive use of his private patients.

Building erected for the purpose to which it is devoted and combines the comforts of a home with the conveniences of a modern hospital.

Located in the residential section, convenient to all parts of the city by means of the street car service.

DR. STUART McGUIRE'S PRIVATE SANATORIUM

¶ Capacity for eighty patients, single and double bedrooms, with or without bath, no wards.

¶ Designed for surgical and gynecological cases. No contagious diseases, insane or colored patients received.

¶ Cost of board and nursing and other information will be obtained by addressing the Secretary.

RICHMOND :-: VIRGINIA

1922 advertisement for St. Luke's Hospital

purpose of undoing the effects of slavery, in the years after it was ratified, the Supreme Court severely limited its ability to do so. The intersection of race and the Fourteenth Amendment is broad and touches on many different issues: segregation in public spaces, schools, and housing; unfair voting laws; laws against marriage between people of different races; and affirmative action. In all these areas, the promise of the Fourteenth Amendment has in many ways never been fully realized.

Separate but Equal

In 1892, Homer Plessy, who was Black, was arrested after refusing to leave the "white car" on a racially segregated train. Plessy's lawyer, a white man named Albion Tourgée, argued that the Louisiana law requiring segregation on train cars violated the Fourteenth Amendment's equal protection clause; one group (white people) was separated from and treated better than another (Black people).

The Supreme Court disagreed. The court held that segregated rail cars were constitutional so long as the different cars were equal—putting the Supreme Court's stamp of approval on the "separate but equal" doctrine that characterized the Jim Crow era.

The court, however, had a very limited idea of what was considered "equal." While separate facilities for Black and white people may have existed, in reality, the facilities that Black people could access were often of lesser quality than those for white people. Black schools, for example, frequently received less funding and had fewer resources than their white counterparts, which meant that Black students did not have the same educational opportunities as white students.

Plessy remained the law until the Supreme Court reversed course in 1954's *Brown v. Board of Education*, which we'll learn about later. Because of the Supreme Court's decision in *Plessy*, Black people were denied educational and job opportunities, as well as goods and services that white people enjoyed; many white employers refused to hire Black people, and many banks refused to give Black people loans. This prevented Black people from building wealth that they could pass on to their descendants, which has ripple effects through today.

ROBERTS V. BOSTON

Although *Plessy* was the first U.S. Supreme Court case about the "separate but equal" doctrine, there's also a Massachusetts Supreme Court case that beat it by more than forty years. In that case, *Roberts v. Boston*, a man named Benjamin Roberts brought a lawsuit to try to desegregate Boston public schools. His daughter, Sarah, was five years old, and he wanted to enroll her in the school closest to their home, which the school committee rules encouraged. But the closest school was only for white students, and the Robertses were Black.

Roberts hired Robert Morris, a Black attorney, and Charles Sumner, a white politician and attorney, to be his lawyers. They argued that "by the constitution and laws of Massachusetts, all persons without distinction of age or sex, birth or color, origin or condition, are equal before the law." (Why didn't Roberts bring his case under the federal Constitution? At the time, there was no Fourteenth Amendment—indeed, the Civil War hadn't even started!)

The Massachusetts Supreme Court ruled against Roberts. Roberts's lawyers had argued that the "maintenance of separate schools tends to deepen and perpetuate the odious distinction of caste, founded in a deep-rooted prejudice in public opinion"—

in other words, that school segregation reinforced the narrative of Black inferiority. But the Massachusetts Supreme Court held that even if that were true, it didn't make the law unconstitutional, because "this prejudice, if it exists, is not created by law, and probably cannot be changed by law."

Roberts and his lawyers had reached a dead end in the courts. They decided to take a different tack and attempt to change public opinion, distributing a pamphlet with the text of the lawyers' court arguments. Their campaign succeeded, and in 1855, the Massachusetts legislature prohibited segregation in public schools. Roberts's story shows us the limits of litigation, and how the solution to many of the problems we'll explore in the next few chapters may well be outside the courts.

Robert Morris

Housing Discrimination

In response to white mob violence in Springfield, Illinois, a group of Black and white activists founded the NAACP in 1909. The organization's goal was to end race discrimination and "secure for all people the rights guaranteed in the 13th, 14th, and 15th Amendments to the United States Constitution."

Not long after its formation, the NAACP decided to challenge a law that prevented Black people in Louisville, Kentucky, from buying homes in majority white neighborhoods (and vice versa). Working with the NAACP, a Black man named William Warley offered to buy a house in a predominantly white neighborhood from a white seller named Charles Buchanan. The Louisville law prevented the sale from being completed, and Buchanan sued. He claimed that the law violated the Fourteenth Amendment's equal protection clause.

The Supreme Court agreed with Buchanan. Even though the court had said in *Plessy* that segregation was constitutional, it explained that this case—*Buchanan v. Warley*—was different. While the plaintiff in *Plessy* could have ridden in a separate rail car, the court wrote, here the Louisville law destroyed "the right of the individual to acquire, enjoy, and dispose of his property." (The court's logic in this case once again ignores that, as we explored above, Jim Crow laws often prevented Black people from acquiring and enjoying property.)

Practically speaking, however, *Buchanan v. Warley* would have little effect, as housing discrimination would continue to occur through what are known as "restrictive covenants." Restrictive covenants are clauses in real estate contracts that put limits on how a property may be used. When such covenants prevent the sale of property to a person of a different race or ethnicity, they are known as *racially* restrictive covenants.

In 1926, the Supreme Court held that racially restrictive covenants were constitutional because they did not involve government actions but instead were agreements between private individuals. (Remember chapter 3, where we learned that the Fourteenth can only protect against government, not private, action.)

That remained the law until the 1940s, when the Supreme Court reconsidered the constitutionality of racially restrictive covenants in *Shelley v. Kraemer.* The Shelleys were a Black family who had bought a house in St. Louis, Missouri, unaware that it had a restrictive covenant in the deed that said it could not be sold to Black people. A white neighbor, Louis Kraemer, sued to prevent the Shelleys from moving in. Based on the 1926 case mentioned on the previous page that said racially restrictive covenants were constitutional—a principle known as stare decisis—Kraemer should have won.

STARE DECISIS

When a court makes a decision, that opinion is binding law. And when other cases are put before that court, the lawyers look to rulings from the past, which are called "precedent." That's why lawyers are always explaining how their case is similar to or different from prior cases—courts usually follow precedent. This is known as stare decisis, Latin for "to stand by things decided."

Now, it's not quite that simple. As we discussed, there are multiple levels of courts in the federal system: district courts, circuit courts, and the Supreme Court. An opinion is only binding on the courts beneath it; for example, while Supreme Court opinions bind the circuit and federal courts, a circuit court opinion only binds the district courts that fall within its geographic boundaries. But! Even if an opinion isn't binding precedent, it can still be persuasive.

Think about it this way: If you're a circuit court, your boss is the Supreme Court. You have to do what it says. But as a circuit court, you're the boss of the district courts that are in your region. If the district courts say you should do something, you can think about it and see if it makes sense to you, but you don't necessarily have to do it. The district courts' opinions are persuasive, not mandatory.

But if you're the boss—aka the Supreme Court—can you ever change your mind? Or do you have to stick with what you said before? Well . . . it depends. If you want to change your mind, you need a *really* good reason—for example, you could say that a lot of things have changed in society since the time the earlier case was decided.

But it gets even more complicated, since there are state courts in addition to federal courts. As we learned way back in chapter 1, federal courts only take a few types of cases—those that are about federal laws and those that are between citizens of different states. State courts, on the other hand, take all sorts of cases.

Like federal courts, there are three levels of state courts: state trial courts, state appellate courts, and state supreme courts. And just as in the federal system, a state court opinion is binding only on the courts beneath it.

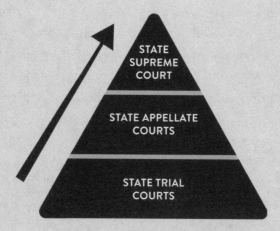

STATE
SUPREME
COURT

STATE APPELLATE
COURTS

STATE TRIAL
COURTS

Court levels in the state system

But here's where it gets *really* messy. Does a state court ever bind a federal court? And does a federal court ever bind a state court?

The answer is, sometimes. State supreme court opinions can be binding on federal courts if the federal court is interpreting state law. And *all* courts—state courts included—are bound by the decisions of the U.S. Supreme Court on issues of federal law.

Confusing as all this is, what it means at the end of the day is

In *Shelley v. Kraemer*, the Supreme Court changed course. Ruling in the Shelleys' favor, the court held that racially restrictive covenants actually *did* violate the equal protection clause because they actually *did* involve government action. Even though the covenants were technically agreements between private parties, a court would have to enforce them. (Like how Kraemer had to sue in court to keep the Shelleys out of the house.) The court getting involved to enforce the covenant was government action, and that government action was unconstitutional. While it wasn't possible to erase racially restrictive covenants entirely, the Supreme Court deprived them of their intended effect by saying they couldn't be enforced.

But the end of racially restrictive covenants did not mean the end of segregated housing. Even without covenants, white people refused to sell their homes to Black people, or made them feel uncomfortable or unsafe after they moved in. Often, wealth disparities caused by decades of systemic racism meant that Black people couldn't afford to buy homes in white neighborhoods, which were frequently more expensive. Even today, Black people applying for home loans are denied at nearly double the rate of white applicants. In these ways—and others—segregated housing has endured and persists to this day.

SYSTEMIC RACISM

Racism is not always obvious, like a job applicant not getting hired because she is Black, or a politician using a racist slur. Systemic racism, sometimes referred to as structural or institutional racism, is a form of racism "pervasively and deeply embedded in systems, laws, written or unwritten policies, and entrenched practices and beliefs." Examples of systemic racism include discriminatory lending policies, unfair policing of people of color, segregated neighborhoods, and unequal school systems.

Despite the civil rights laws of the 1960s, racial inequities persist because of these "deeply rooted, unfair systems that sustain the legacy of former overtly discriminatory practices, policies, laws, and beliefs." As author and journalist Ta-Nehisi Coates explains in his essay "The Case for Reparations":

> An honest assessment of America's relationship to the black family reveals the country to be not its nurturer but its destroyer.
>
> And this destruction did not end with slavery. Discriminatory laws joined the equal burden of citizenship to unequal distribution of its bounty. These laws reached their apex in the mid-20th century, when the federal government—through housing policies—engineered the wealth gap, which remains with us to this day. When we think of white supremacy, we picture Colored Only signs, but we should picture pirate flags.

Policies like racially restrictive covenants may no longer be legal, but the systems they set in motion persist to this day and perpetuate the oppression of people of color.

The Right to Vote

Many Black people were denied their right to vote during the Jim Crow era, both by voter intimidation—where white people would threaten and often harm Black people for exercising their right to vote—and by discriminatory voting laws.

The Fifteenth Amendment said that the right to vote "shall not be denied or abridged by the United States or by any State on account of race, color, or previous condition of servitude," which meant voting laws couldn't explicitly exclude people based on their race. So Black voting was instead suppressed by what are known as "laws of pretense." Laws of pretense say they're doing one thing, like making sure voters are "qualified" to vote, but really do another, like preventing Black people from voting.

These laws of pretense took many forms, including poll taxes, which required that voters pay a certain sum of money in order to cast a ballot. People who could not afford the fee, who were disproportionately Black, were not allowed to vote. Other laws established literacy tests, which said that a voter had to "understand" the state constitution. These tests were administered unfairly to Black people, often by white people who wanted to prevent them from voting.

Many of these laws had "grandfather clauses," which said you didn't have to pay a poll tax or take a literacy test if your grandfather could have voted in 1866. But the Fifteenth Amendment, which guaranteed Black men the right to vote, wasn't passed until 1870—which meant you could qualify for this exception only if you were white.

In 1915's *Guinn v. United States*, the NAACP sued to challenge Oklahoma's grandfather clause as a violation of the Fifteenth Amendment. The clause at issue said that voters did not have to take a literacy test if they descended from a "person who was, on January 1, 1866, or any time prior thereto, entitled to vote"—that is, if they descended from a white person. The Supreme Court struck the clause down, explaining that the court knew exactly what the state was trying to do: "How can there be room for any serious dispute concerning the repugnancy of the standard based upon January 1, 1866 (a date which preceded the adoption of the Fifteenth Amendment) . . . ?" Setting the date before Black people were allowed to vote, the court explained, made clear that the Oklahoma lawmakers were intentionally targeting Black voters.

But even without grandfather clauses, states continued to discriminate against Black voters using poll taxes and literacy tests. Poll taxes persisted until the mid-1960s, when the Twenty-Fourth Amendment abolished their use in federal elections and the Supreme Court declared them unconstitutional under the Fourteenth Amendment. And literacy tests continued until Congress outlawed them in the Voting Rights Act of 1965.

Today, states are attacking voting in different ways, including by restricting early voting and mail-in ballots, imposing voter ID requirements, and limiting voting hours and the number of polling places. Georgia even banned handing out water or snacks to people waiting in line to vote.

Like poll taxes and literacy tests, these are laws of pretense. While they do not directly target people based on their race, they are intended to prevent people of color (specifically Black people) from voting. These laws all have one purpose: They make it harder to vote. When voting is harder, this disproportionately affects people who have fewer resources—like people who can't afford to take a day off work or who can't drive to a faraway polling site. And because of centuries of slavery, Jim Crow, and systemic racism, people with fewer resources are more likely to be people of color, and specifically Black.

The lawmakers who pass these voting restrictions are aware of all this—it is why they are doing it in the first place. In a 2021 opinion striking down a voter ID law, for example, a North Carolina trial court concluded that the law "was motivated at least in part by an unconstitutional intent to target African American voters." Just as in the Jim Crow era, these are laws of pretense: Lawmakers say they're "preventing fraud," when they're really trying to keep the voting rolls white.

Equality in Education

The Fourteenth Amendment was also used to fight for racial equality in education. In 1936's *Murray v. Pearson*, the highest court in Maryland considered whether a law school could exclude people based on their race. Donald Murray, a Black man who lived in Maryland, wanted to attend the University of Maryland Law School, but it admitted only white people. Murray brought suit to challenge the law school's discrimination as a violation of the Fourteenth Amendment right to equal protection.

Murray's lawyer was a man named Thurgood Marshall, who would go on to represent the Shelleys before the U.S. Supreme Court in 1948 and eventually become the first Black Supreme Court justice. In fact, Marshall had a very personal connection to the case: He, too, had been unable to attend the Maryland state law school because he was Black. Marshall went to law school at Howard University, a historically Black university in Washington, D.C., instead. The dean of Howard Law School, a Black lawyer named Charles Hamilton Houston, mentored Marshall and helped him bring Murray's case. They hoped this case about law school would be a stepping stone toward ensuring equality in college and K–12 education as well.

In *Murray*, the Maryland court said that being forced to go to law school out of state instead of in Maryland wasn't "separate but equal"—attending school farther from home would be more expensive, plus it wasn't fair to make someone learn law in a state where they didn't plan to practice. As the court wrote:

> To attend Howard University the petitioner, living in
> Baltimore, would be under the necessity of paying the
> expenses of daily travel to and fro, with some expenses while
> in Washington, or of removing to Washington to live during
> his law school education, and to pay the incidental expenses
> of thus living away from home; whereas in Baltimore,
> living at home, he would have no traveling expenses, and
> comparatively small living expenses . . . And as the petitioner
> points out, he could not there have the advantages of study
> of the law of this state primarily, and of attendance on state
> courts, where he intends to practice.

Though it applied only in Maryland and not nationally, *Murray v. Pearson* started chipping away at the "separate but equal" doctrine. Courts started taking a hard look at whether separate facilities were indeed equal.

The NAACP ultimately attacked the idea of "separate but equal" at its core in *Brown v. Board of Education of Topeka*, which sought to integrate public schools in Topeka, Kansas. Working with other notable Black lawyers like Constance Baker Motley and Pauli Murray, Thurgood Marshall argued that segregation sends the message of Black inferiority and white supremacy. "Witnesses testified that segregation deterred the development of the personalities of these children," he told the Supreme Court in 1952. "The summation of that testimony is that the Negro children have road blocks put up in their minds as a result of this segregation, so that the amount of education that they take in is much less than other students take in."

But Marshall did not represent the views of many Black people at the time, including many Black people in Topeka. As Charise Cheney, an associate professor in the department of Indigenous, Race, and Ethnic Studies at the University of Oregon, explains, many Black Topekans were "concerned that destroying all-black schools would undermine the quality of black education." Numerous Black schools in Topeka incorporated Black culture into their missions, whether by teaching Black history or beginning each school day with the Negro National Anthem, and teachers in these schools were extremely dedicated to their students. Black students "had access to equitable facilities and funding" as compared to white students, which was unique among Black public schools at the time.

Nevertheless, in *Brown*, the Supreme Court agreed with the NAACP, holding that forced segregation violated the Fourteenth Amendment's equal protection clause. The court explained that separate educational facilities were inherently unequal:

> *We conclude that, in the field of public education, the doctrine of "separate but equal" has no place. Separate educational facilities are inherently unequal. Therefore, we hold that the plaintiffs and others similarly situated for whom the actions have been brought are, by reason of the segregation complained of, deprived of the equal protection of the laws guaranteed by the Fourteenth Amendment.*

To reach this conclusion, the court had to explicitly overturn *Plessy v. Ferguson*. The only difference between *Plessy* and *Brown*, however, was that time had passed, and the composition of the Supreme Court had changed. There was no argument made in *Brown* that hadn't been made in *Plessy*.

Thurgood Marshall, center, with two of his fellow attorneys
(George Edward Chalmer Hayes, left, and James Nabrit, right)
after winning Brown v. Board of Education.

Despite the *Brown* decision, change was slow to come. Prince Edward County, Virginia, for example, closed its public schools for five years rather than integrate them.

And even where integration did occur, it was implemented in ways that hurt Black students. School boards and state legislators shut down numerous all-Black schools, choosing to integrate the white schools instead. This reflected the racial prejudices of the people in power, but it also was in line with the way Marshall argued *Brown*: He said that Black people were harmed by being separated from white people, not that white people were harmed by being separated from Black people.

In these formerly all-white schools, Black students "were subjected to physical violence and emotional abuse, racial intimidation and hostility and illegal suspensions." What's more, many Black teachers and principals lost their jobs after *Brown*, as "racial prejudice prohibited them from following Black students into integrated schools." Leslie T. Fenwick, professor and former dean of the Howard University School of Education, calculates that "100,000 Black principals and teachers were shunted off the payrolls due to white resistance to *Brown*, leaving Black educators nearly $1 billion poorer." The aftermath of *Brown* shows us that even when the Supreme Court rules in a way that seems pro-equality, those rulings can still have harmful effects.

In the years that followed *Brown*, the Supreme Court decided several other cases that upheld school integration. In 1968, the court held in *Green v. County School Board of New Kent County* that a "freedom of choice" plan, where students could pick which school they wanted to go to, violated the equal protection clause because the schools remained segregated even after the plan was implemented. The court acknowledged that "freedom of choice" could work in some circumstances, but explained that the school administration needed to create a plan that would lead to desegregation. Three years later, in 1971, the court held in *Swann v. Charlotte-Mecklenburg Board of Education* that having students travel by bus to schools farther from their homes was an acceptable way to integrate schools.

But in 1974, with two new conservative justices on the bench, the court changed course. In *Milliken v. Bradley*, the Supreme Court ruled that students from the predominantly white suburbs of Detroit could not be forced to integrate with students from the city, which was predominantly Black. As we learned earlier in this chapter, segregated housing is no accident but is instead based on decades of systemic racism. *Milliken* thus "limited the reach of *Brown* by making clear that desegregation would not touch the suburbs," explains James Ryan, the former dean of the Harvard Graduate School of Education. "As a result, the education of urban and suburban students remains a world apart."

Indeed, segregated schooling persists to this day: A 2022 study from the U.S. Government Accountability Office shows that the nation's public schools "remain divided along racial, ethnic, and economic lines," with more than a third of students attending a school that was primarily one race or ethnicity. While we might think segregation would be more prevalent in the South because of its history of Jim Crow laws, that same report found that the most segregated schools today are in the Northeast and Midwest.

THE CIVIL RIGHTS MOVEMENT

Emmett Till was a Black kid from Chicago spending the summer in Mississippi with his family. On August 28, 1955, fourteen-year-old

Till was murdered by two white men. His alleged crime? A white woman in a grocery store named Carolyn Bryant said that he had insulted her. He was just there to buy candy.

As punishment for his supposed crime, Bryant's husband and brother-in-law kidnapped Till, beating him before shooting him in the head and throwing his body in the Tallahatchie River. Three days later, his body was discovered, grossly mutilated.

Mamie Till, Emmett's mother, brought his body home to Chicago and insisted on an open casket funeral. She "wanted the world to see what those men had done to her son." She wanted to show them the true nature of racism in America.

Photos of Emmett's mutilated body were published in *Jet* magazine and the *Chicago Defender*, a Black newspaper. The murder made headlines worldwide; a Belgian newspaper, for example, published an article called "Racism in the USA: A young black is lynched in Mississippi."

Still, Emmett's killers went free. They were found not guilty of murder by an all-white, all-male jury after Bryant testified on the stand that Till had grabbed and threatened her. Just months after their acquittal the two men described for *Look* magazine exactly how they had committed the murder. But it would be another *fifty years* before Bryant admitted that she had lied to the jury about what Till had said and done to her.

Barely one hundred days after Emmett Till's murder, a forty-two-year-old tailor by the name of Rosa Parks was arrested for refusing to give up her seat to a white passenger on a bus in Montgomery, Alabama. Years later, she would meet Mamie Till. "Rosa Parks would tell me how she felt about Emmett," Mamie Till later wrote, "how she had thought about him on that fateful day when she took that historic stand by keeping her seat."

Parks's action that day on the bus was strategic, tied not only to the murder of Emmett Till but also to generations of racial injustice; it was part of the growing civil rights movement of the mid-twentieth century, which sought to secure equal rights for Black Americans. Indeed, Black people in Montgomery had long considered boycotting the bus system. Nine months earlier, a Black teenager named Claudette Colvin also refused to give up her seat to a white person.

Parks's arrest helped the modern-day civil rights movement gain broader visibility. After she was arrested, the Black community organized a bus boycott, and they asked a little-known twenty-six-year-old preacher to help lead it: Dr. Martin Luther King Jr.

King would become one of the most important figures in the civil rights movement. He had been a pastor at a Baptist church in Montgomery for about a year before he was asked to lead the bus boycotts, and he soon became well known for advancing civil rights through nonviolent resistance.

Dr. Martin Luther King Jr. at a press conference in 1964

Other important figures during the civil rights era include Bayard Rustin, an adviser of King's who was once arrested because he was gay and later advocated for LGBTQ+ rights; Fannie Lou Hamer, a cofounder of the Mississippi Freedom Democratic Party and organizer of the Freedom Summer, which aimed to help Black people register to vote; and Malcolm X. Malcolm X criticized King's focus on nonviolence and urged Black people to defend themselves "by any means necessary." He "argued that more was at stake than the civil right to sit in a restaurant or even to vote—the most important issues were Black identity, integrity, and independence."

During the civil rights era, several landmark laws were passed. The Civil Rights Act of 1964 banned employment discrimination on the basis of race, color, religion, sex, or national origin and banned segregation in public places. And the Voting Rights Act of 1965 sought to address barriers to Black voting. But as we've seen throughout this chapter, racial discrimination has persisted despite these laws, and the work of fighting for civil rights continues today.

Interracial Marriage

Marriage is more than just a ceremony or tradition, and its effects go beyond the personal or community level; the government gives legal protections to married people. Before the Civil War, enslaved Black people had no right to marry and could be separated from partners and children against their will at any time. Only after the Civil War, with the protections of the Fourteenth Amendment, could Black people marry one another. Still, they could not marry people of another race because of miscegenation laws, which prevented people of different races from having sex, living together, or getting married.

In 1883's *Pace v. Alabama*, the Supreme Court considered whether one such law violated the equal protection clause of the Constitution. In that case, Tony Pace, who was Black, and Mary Cox, who was white, were convicted under Alabama's miscegenation law "for living together in a state of adultery or fornication" as people of different races. After being sentenced to two years in prison, they appealed to the U.S. Supreme Court.

The court affirmed their convictions, holding that the Alabama law didn't violate the Fourteenth Amendment's equal protection clause because it punished Black and white people equally for violating it: "Whatever discrimination is made in the punishment prescribed in the two sections is directed against the offense designated, and not against the person of any particular color or race. The punishment of each offending person, whether white or black, is the same."

This didn't make much sense. Of course the Alabama law discriminated on the basis of race—white people could marry white people, but they couldn't marry people of other races. The fact that Black and white people were punished equally simply meant that the law wasn't *doubly* discriminatory.

Still, *Pace* remained the law until 1967's *Loving v. Virginia*. In that case, the Supreme Court considered whether a Virginia law that criminalized interracial marriage was constitutional. The court explained the facts of the case:

> *In June 1958, two residents of Virginia, Mildred Jeter, a Negro woman, and Richard Loving, a white man, were married in the District of Columbia pursuant to its laws. Shortly after their marriage, the Lovings returned to Virginia and established their marital abode in Caroline County. At the October Term, 1958, of the Circuit Court of Caroline County, a grand jury issued an indictment charging the Lovings with violating Virginia's ban on interracial marriages. On January 6, 1959, the Lovings pleaded guilty to the charge and were sentenced to one year in jail; however, the trial judge suspended the sentence for a period of 25 years on the condition that the Lovings leave the State and not return to Virginia together for 25 years.*

Because they were of different races, the Lovings would either have to serve a year in jail or leave their home and state for at least twenty-five years.

Mildred and Richard Loving

The Lovings challenged the Virginia law as a violation of their Fourteenth Amendment equal protection rights, making the exact same argument that Tony Pace and Mary Cox had made in the 1800s. The state's argument in response echoed the holding in *Pace*: "Because its miscegenation statutes punish equally both the white and the Negro participants in an interracial marriage, these statutes, despite their reliance on racial classifications, do not constitute an invidious discrimination based upon race."

This time, the Supreme Court ruled differently and struck down the Virginia law. Again, what had changed in the intervening years was the composition of the court. In *Loving*, the Supreme

Court reversed its holding in *Pace*, explaining that even though the law punished Black and white people equally, it nevertheless rested "solely upon distinctions drawn according to race" because it proscribed "generally accepted conduct if engaged in by members of different races." Which is to say, white people could marry other white people, but they could not marry people of other races, and that was racial discrimination.

Because the Virginia law discriminated on the basis of race, the Supreme Court had to take a hard look at whether there was any "compelling state interest" that made the law necessary. This is what's known as "strict scrutiny."

TIERS OF SCRUTINY

The equal protection clause isn't just about race—it applies to *any* distinctions drawn by the government. For example, if a law said "people who have brown hair must wear glasses or contacts when they drive," you'd have a pretty good argument that the law violated the equal protection clause. Why on earth is hair color relevant to driving safety?

But if that law said "people who fail a vision test must wear glasses or contacts when they drive," it would probably be fine. In that case, the distinction at issue (vision test results) is clearly related to the law (about driving safety).

The court looks more skeptically at certain sorts of classifications, like those based on a person's race or gender. This is because it's really unlikely that a distinction based on these categories would actually have a legitimate relationship to a law. (Like the race-based Black codes—there's absolutely no reason Black people should be subject to those restrictions based on the color of their skin.)

When the court is looking at a law that distinguishes based

on race, national origin (what country you're from), or religion, it applies "strict scrutiny." This means that the court is taking a hard look at the law in question—and making sure that the classification is very closely related to the purpose of the law—because the distinction at issue makes the court skeptical. While this doesn't necessarily mean the law will be held unconstitutional, it is very likely.

For reasons that we'll explore in chapter 8, distinctions based on gender are reviewed a little less closely—what's known as "intermediate scrutiny."

Distinctions that aren't based on one of these protected groups are reviewed at a lower level: The court asks if the lawmakers had a "rational basis," or logical reason, for distinguishing between the groups. In the example above, a court would likely find that a law that distinguished based on hair color had no rational relationship to driving safety.

These three levels—strict, intermediate, and rational basis—are often referred to as the "tiers of scrutiny."

Applying strict scrutiny, the Supreme Court struck down the Virginia miscegenation law as a violation of equal protection. The court held that the law's real purpose was "invidious racial discrimination," since "the fact that Virginia prohibits only interracial marriages involving white persons demonstrates that the racial classifications must stand on their own justification, as measures designed to maintain White Supremacy."

While *Loving v. Virginia* ensured that people could marry someone of another race, interracial couples still face discrimination today—ranging from disapproval to public assaults. *Loving* also assumed that married couples were heterosexual. In chapter 10, we'll learn about the fight for marriage equality for LGBTQ+ people.

Affirmative Action

In the wake of the civil rights movement, many colleges and universities began to try to make up for the disadvantages Black people faced in their admissions processes. This is what's known as affirmative action. Given the history of racial discrimination in the United States—discrimination that continues to this day—some schools considered race a "plus factor" in the admissions process. Other schools implemented race quotas, requiring that a certain number of people of different races be admitted each year.

In 1978, one such race quota system was challenged in *Regents of the University of California v. Bakke.* In that case, Allan Bakke, who was white, didn't get accepted into the medical school at the University of California, Davis. He believed that the only reason he was rejected was because the school used race-based quotas. So he sued the university, arguing that its quota system violated the Fourteenth Amendment's equal protection clause.

The case made its way to the Supreme Court, which ruled in Bakke's favor. The court said that race discrimination is race discrimination, regardless of whether it's being done for positive reasons (like trying to remedy historical discrimination through affirmative action) or negative ones (like preventing Black people from voting). But this view of racial discrimination—known as the color blindness doctrine—fails to account for the history of racism in America. Laws or policies that try to help historically disadvantaged racial groups are not the same as laws that try to harm those groups, and yet the Supreme Court views them identically. Cases like these show us the limits of law and "how difficult it is to deal with these demands according to traditional legal doctrines."

The court in *Bakke* said there was only one way affirmative action could be constitutional: It was okay to select an incoming class with diversity in mind, as long as formal quota systems weren't used. This played out in 2003's *Grutter v. Bollinger*, in which the Supreme Court said that the University of Michigan Law School's race-conscious admissions program—which considered race as a factor when admitting students, but didn't have a quota system—was constitutional. The court ruled similarly in 2016's *Fisher v. University of Texas*, upholding the University of Texas at Austin's affirmative action policy for undergraduate admissions.

That all changed in 2023, when a group called Students for Fair Admissions brought a set of lawsuits challenging the affirmative action programs at Harvard College and the University of North Carolina. In June of that year, the Supreme Court ruled 6–3 in favor of the plaintiffs, holding that affirmative action in college admissions violated the Fourteenth Amendment's equal protection clause. "Eliminating racial discrimination means eliminating all of it," the majority wrote. "The student must be treated based on his or her experiences as an individual—not on the basis of race."

Dissenting from the majority opinion, Justice Ketanji Brown Jackson explained that the court's reasoning was flawed because "our country has never been colorblind. Given the lengthy history of state-sponsored race-based preferences in America, to say that anyone is now victimized if a college considered whether that legacy of discrimination has unequally advantaged its applicants fails to acknowledge the well-documented 'intergenerational transmission of inequality' that still plagues our citizenry." Affirmative action programs were designed to help address that inequality, but the court had discarded them in the name of equal protection.

In ruling affirmative action unconstitutional, the court also discarded decades of precedent, including *Fisher v. University of Texas*, which it had decided less than a decade prior. As we've seen time and time again, the difference here is simply that the composition of the court has changed, and several new justices with more conservative viewpoints have joined the bench.

The Fourteenth Amendment has been a deeply incomplete solution to the problems it sought to address. Segregated housing and segregated education persist despite Supreme Court rulings aimed at addressing them; lawmakers continue to limit the right to vote; and affirmative action is no longer permissible in college admissions processes. And as we'll see later, antidiscrimination laws—which protect people from, for example, being fired on the basis of their race—may not be the best basis to seek equality, either.

This chapter shows us the limits of the law, and that solutions moving forward may instead lie in other areas, like community activism and organizing. Some organizations today that work to advance racial equality outside the courts include the Marsha P. Johnson Institute, which works to protect the rights of Black transgender people "by organizing our community, advocating for our people, creating an intentional healing community, developing transformative leadership, and promoting our collective power"; the Marshall Project, a news organization that focuses on the U.S. criminal legal system; and Black Lives Matter, an organization whose work includes digital activism, advocacy for policy change, on-the-ground organizing, supporting Black artists, building healing spaces for Black communities, and supporting research and education on prison abolition and Black history curricula. For these organizations and others like them, the fight to uphold the rights enshrined in the Fourteenth Amendment need not happen in the courts.

In the next chapter, we'll take a look at how the Fourteenth Amendment was eventually extended to cover gender discrimination, before turning to its role in immigration and LGBTQ+ rights.

The Fight for Gender Equality

Myra Bradwell, a white woman, had studied law and applied to join the Illinois bar in 1869. She was rejected because of her gender, and she sued over her denial, arguing to the Supreme Court that she had been denied equal protection of the laws under the Fourteenth Amendment.

When the Fourteenth Amendment was passed, its drafters were thinking about race, not gender. Soon, however, its protections—

Myra Bradwell

including both the equal protection and due process clauses—would come to apply to women as well. Though some may argue that in the years after 1954 the Supreme Court enlarged the Fourteenth Amendment "beyond recognition," in reality the Fourteenth Amendment has struggled to address gender discrimination, and there remains much work to be done outside the courts.

Expanding Equal Protection

In 1872, the day after it decided the *Slaughterhouse Cases* (which we discussed in chapter 4), the Supreme Court decided Myra Bradwell's case.

Bradwell lost spectacularly. The Supreme Court held that the practice of law by any citizen was not a privilege or immunity protected by the Fourteenth Amendment. In a separate concurring opinion, three justices went further, saying that a woman had "no legal existence" apart from her husband, and that the "paramount destiny" of a woman is "to fulfill the noble and benign offices of wife and mother." (Remember from "Law School 101" that a concurring opinion is one that supports the majority's ultimate decision but for different reasons.) Because women were naturally different from men, the concurring justices explained, the state was allowed to discriminate against them, including by barring them from the practice of law.

The prevailing philosophy of the time was of "separate spheres": Women belonged at home, with children, while men belonged out in the world. Before 1839, when states slowly began enacting married women's property laws, a wife had no legal rights outside the existence of her husband. In many states, a married woman couldn't own property, open a bank account, or serve on a jury. This was based on the legal doctrine called "coverture"—the husband's identity "covered" the wife's. Indeed, a husband and wife were usually given one U.S. passport in the husband's name.

When learning about cases like *Bradwell*, it's important to consider how these laws affected women of different races and classes in different ways. Thinking about how multiple parts of one's identity (like race, gender, and class) intersect is often referred to as "intersectionality." While the term "intersectionality" was coined by law professor Kimberlé Crenshaw in 1989, the concept existed for many years before then, including in the speeches and writings of Sojourner Truth, a Black abolitionist and women's rights advocate who escaped slavery in 1826, and the writings of the Combahee River Collective, a group of Black feminists in Boston in the 1970s. Applying an intersectional lens to *Bradwell*, we might consider how this case advanced an issue—becoming a lawyer—that was important primarily to white, wealthy women. As we discussed in previous chapters, Black people at this time were subject to lynchings, violence, and the Black codes—all issues that threatened their livelihoods more directly than what Myra Bradwell was fighting for.

In the years after *Bradwell*, the Fourteenth Amendment continued to be of little use in the women's equality movement. For example, in 1908, the Supreme Court upheld an Oregon law limiting the number of hours women could work, and in 1948, the court upheld a Michigan law that said women couldn't be licensed bartenders unless they were wives or daughters of male owners. In both these cases, the court said there was good reason to treat women differently than men, and so the equal protection clause had not been violated. Laws like these were supposedly meant to "protect" women, but in reality, they kept women subordinate.

Over time, colleges began admitting women (though medical schools and law schools did not). But this was via grassroots political action, not litigation; any time a plaintiff brought an equal protection challenge to a law that discriminated against women, the Supreme Court would say that there was good reason to treat women differently from men. As for Myra Bradwell herself, she was ultimately admitted to the Illinois bar in 1890, but no thanks to the Fourteenth Amendment: This was only after the state passed a law allowing women to practice law.

WOMEN'S SUFFRAGE AND THE NINETEENTH AMENDMENT

Born in 1820, Susan B. Anthony was a famous advocate for women's suffrage (remember, "suffrage" means the right to vote). While many Black women had also advocated for this right—including Ida B. Wells, who we discussed in chapter 4—the suffrage movement that Anthony led was very white, and Anthony and other white suffragists held the racist belief that Black men were less deserving of the vote than white women. Often, the white suffragists did not let Black women march with them—or if they did, the Black women had to march at the end of the line. At

Susan B. Anthony

a 1913 march, however, Wells flouted organizers' request that she march at the end of the parade and instead took her position with the rest of the Illinois contingent.

In the 1872 election, Anthony convinced fourteen other women in Rochester to vote along with her, despite the fact that they weren't legally allowed to. This was no small request: They could be punished by up to three years in prison and a $500 fine for voting without a legal right.

The women cast their ballots and were later arrested; Anthony was arrested and fined $100, but refused to pay. The court chose not to imprison her for her refusal to pay the fine, which prevented Anthony from appealing the case and possibly taking the issue to the Supreme Court. But even if she had appealed, arguing that her equal protection rights had been violated, her case likely would have come out like Myra Bradwell's; it would be a century before the Fourteenth Amendment came to apply to discrimination based on gender.

It wasn't until 1920 that women finally won the right to vote with the Nineteenth Amendment. That amendment reads: "The right of citizens of the United States to vote shall not be denied or abridged by the United States or by any State on account of sex."

The 1970s saw the rise of the women's liberation movement. Some in the movement pushed for the Equal Rights Amendment, which would put women's equality directly into the Constitution since the Fourteenth didn't seem to protect them. Others took a different view, once again demanding that the existing Fourteenth Amendment should be interpreted to protect women. Pauli Murray—a Black lawyer who had a hand in *Brown v. Board of Education*, which we discussed in chapter 7—knew that the Fourteenth hadn't worked for women before, but also knew that times (and the justices) had changed. Murray drew an analogy between gender and race discrimination, explaining that both discriminated against people based on characteristics they couldn't change.

Pauli Murray

Another lawyer named Ruth Bader Ginsburg—who would later become the first Jewish woman to serve on the Supreme Court—adopted Murray's argument in her cases about discrimination against women. In 1971's *Reed v. Reed*, Ginsburg argued that an Idaho law that said "males must be preferred to females" in naming estate administrators violated the Fourteenth Amendment's equal protection clause. (An estate administrator is a person who serves as the legal representative of a person who has died, collecting and distributing the deceased person's assets.) Murray was listed as an honorary coauthor on Ginsburg's brief in recognition of the legal theories Murray had helped develop.

In considering the Idaho law, the Supreme Court applied rational basis scrutiny. As we learned in chapter 7, "scrutiny" means, basically, *How hard should the court look at this law?* When a court applies rational basis scrutiny, it asks only if there is any logical reason behind the law. In *Reed*, the court determined that there was no such logical reason, explaining that the law's mandatory preference for men over women was "the very kind of arbitrary legislative choice forbidden by the Equal Protection Clause of the Fourteenth Amendment."

Ruth Bader Ginsburg in 1977

Two years later, in 1973's *Frontiero v. Richardson*, Ginsburg challenged a federal law that said the husband of a woman in the military couldn't get dependent benefits, but the wife of a man in the military could. Ginsburg argued that such sex-based classifications were "suspect" (meaning questionable) and required close scrutiny under equal protection principles. It was important to Ginsburg for the court to view gender-based classifications with something more than rational basis scrutiny—the more closely the court looked at the law, the more likely that it would be held unconstitutional.

The Supreme Court struck down the federal law, holding that male and female military personnel should get equal dependency benefits. The court, however, didn't agree on what level of scrutiny should apply when distinctions are based on gender. Distinctions based on race are reviewed under strict scrutiny, which means very closely. How closely should the court look at laws about gender?

The Supreme Court answered that question in a 1976 case called *Craig v. Boren*, which concerned an Oklahoma law that said women could buy beer at the age of eighteen but men had to wait until they were twenty-one. The court explained that there were differences between men and women that made it okay to distinguish between them sometimes (though not always). So rather than apply strict scrutiny, it would apply something a bit less intense—intermediate scrutiny.

Using that standard, the court considered the state's explanation of why Oklahoma's law was necessary: that young men were more likely to drink and drive. The court rejected that argument, explaining that it "does not satisfy us that sex represents a legitimate, accurate proxy for the regulation of drinking and driving"—in other words, that a person's gender did not determine whether they would drive drunk—and striking down the law as a violation of the Fourteenth Amendment.

Today, equal protection arguments are made in many cases when the government discriminates on the basis of gender. In 2017's *Sessions v. Morales-Santana*, for example, the Supreme Court considered whether a federal law that created different citizenship requirements based on gender violated the equal protection rights contained in the Fifth Amendment. (Because the law in question was federal, this case involved the Fifth Amendment, not the Fourteenth. Even though the Fifth Amendment doesn't explicitly say the words "equal protection," the Supreme Court has explained that its due process clause encompasses the right to equal protection, and that "equal protection analysis in the Fifth Amendment area is the same as that under the Fourteenth Amendment.")

The federal law at issue in *Sessions v. Morales-Santana* said that a child born abroad to a citizen parent and a noncitizen parent had to meet different requirements to become a U.S. citizen themselves, depending on whether the citizen parent was the mom or dad. An unwed U.S. citizen mother could pass citizenship to her child born abroad if she had lived in the U.S. continuously for only a year. But an unwed father had to have lived in the U.S. continuously for five years. As the Supreme Court explained, these differing requirements were based on the inappropriate stereotype that unwed citizen mothers were "natural" guardians, but unwed citizen fathers "would care little about, and have scant contact with, their nonmarital children." Because the government failed to advance any "exceedingly persuasive" justification for these gender-based distinctions, the law violated the Constitution's equal protection requirement.

The equal protection clause has also helped protect trans people from discrimination. In 2020's *Grimm v. Gloucester County School*

Board, a trans male student named Gavin Grimm sued his school for refusing to let him use the boys' restroom and won. The circuit court held that the school's bathroom policy violated the equal protection clause because it discriminated on the basis of sex. Other courts have held that laws banning trans women from playing on women's sports teams and laws preventing trans people from getting gender-affirming care also violate the equal protection clause.

The Eighth Circuit Court of Appeals, for example, held in *Brandt v. Rutledge* that an Arkansas law banning gender-affirming care for trans minors unconstitutionally discriminated on the basis of sex. (Gender-affirming care "encompasses a range of social, psychological, behavioral, and medical interventions 'designed to support and affirm an individual's gender identity' when it conflicts with the gender they were assigned at birth," explains the American Association of Medical Colleges. Such interventions may include counseling, hormone therapy, and, in some cases, surgery.) The court explained that "medical procedures that are permitted for a minor of one sex are prohibited for a minor of another sex": a minor assigned male at birth may be prescribed testosterone, but a minor assigned female at birth may not. For this reason, the court concluded, the Arkansas law violated the equal protection clause.

After *Brandt,* other courts uniformly held that similar bans on gender-affirming care were unconstitutional. But that changed in July and August 2023, when the Sixth and Eleventh Circuit Courts of Appeals both preliminarily upheld the constitutionality of bans on gender-affirming care for minors. As of this writing, neither of these cases has been ruled on by the Supreme Court, which has the ability decide the constitutionality of such bans nationwide. Given the conservative composition of the court, legal commentators worry that wins for trans rights in the lower courts may be short-lived.

BUSH V. GORE

One surprising instance where the Fourteenth Amendment's equal protection clause came into play was the 2000 case of *Bush v. Gore*. Republican George W. Bush and Democrat Al Gore were locked in a very close presidential election, with the state of Florida as the tiebreaker. Gore requested a recount in several Florida counties because the numbers were so close.

In a 7–2 ruling, the Supreme Court held that the recount violated the equal protection clause because different Florida counties had different counting standards. Because this distinction wasn't based on a suspect class like race or gender, the court considered only whether there was a "rational basis" for the distinction, concluding that there was not.

But rather than order every county to use the same standards, the court said in a 5–4 decision that the recount had to stop altogether because there wasn't enough time for the counties to start over before the deadline. Before the recount, Bush had been in the lead—so this decision ensured that Bush, a Republican, won, and Gore, a Democrat, lost.

The majority of the Supreme Court justices at the time had been nominated by Republicans, and this ruling made it seem like they had made a political decision. As one legal scholar put it, "It is no secret that the Supreme Court's decision in *Bush v. Gore* has shaken the faith of many legal academics in the Supreme Court." But as we've seen throughout this book, the Supreme Court's decisions have always been political.

Reproductive Rights and Justice

Access to reproductive health care, including contraception and abortion, is essential for full equality. For people to be able to achieve their goals—whether that's getting a job, going to school, traveling, or whatever else they want to do with their lives—they have to be able to control whether and when they have children. Beyond that, it is a fundamental human right to be able to determine for oneself, without state interference, whether to become a parent.

REPRODUCTION, SEX, AND GENDER

Reproductive rights are often discussed as a "women's issue." While it is true that many laws limiting reproductive rights are targeted at and based on stereotypes about women, not all people who get pregnant, and not all people who need reproductive health care, are women. A transgender man can have a uterus, as can a genderqueer, gender fluid, nonbinary, or gender nonconforming person. This means that trans men, genderqueer, gender fluid, nonbinary, and gender nonconforming people can all get pregnant. It's important to keep this in mind throughout this discussion of reproductive rights, as many of the cases we discuss refer only to pregnant women.

Definitions from the Human Rights Campaign Foundation:

- **genderqueer**: People who reject static categories of gender and may also embrace a fluidity of sexual orientation. People who identify as genderqueer may see themselves as both male and female, somewhere in between, or completely outside these categories.
- **gender fluid**: People who do not identify with a single fixed gender or who have an unfixed gender identity.
- **gender nonconforming**: People whose gender expression does not conform to the traditional expectations of their gender or fit neatly into a category. While many also identify as transgender, not all gender nonconforming people do.
- **nonbinary**: People who do not identify exclusively as a man or a

woman. Nonbinary people may identify as being both a man and a woman, somewhere in between, or completely outside these categories. While many also identify as transgender, not all nonbinary people do. Nonbinary can also encompass identities such as genderqueer or gender fluid.

· **transgender** or **trans**: People whose gender identity or expression is different from cultural expectations based on the sex they were assigned at birth. (Compare with **cisgender** or **cis**: People whose gender identity or expression corresponds with cultural expectations based on the sex they were assigned at birth.)

While the ability to control reproductive outcomes is linked to equality, the Supreme Court came to view it through a different legal theory: privacy. The privacy doctrine began with the 1965 case of *Griswold v. Connecticut*, which concerned a Connecticut law that prohibited the use of birth control. Estelle Griswold, a white woman who was executive director of the Planned Parenthood League of Connecticut, was arrested and convicted under the law for providing birth control. She appealed, arguing that the law violated the constitutional rights of married women.

Writing for the majority, Justice William Douglas ruled in Griswold's favor. He explained that the Connecticut law violated marital privacy: Why should the state be able to decide what married couples did in their bedrooms? Although privacy is not listed as a right in the Constitution, Douglas explained that it was assumed—otherwise, other rights (like the Third Amendment right not to quarter soldiers in one's home) didn't make sense. He then connected this privacy right to the Fourteenth Amendment's due process clause, which says the government cannot "deprive any

Griswold outside the Planned Parenthood clinic in New Haven, Connecticut

person of life, liberty, or property, without due process of law."

In previous chapters we've discussed what's known as "procedural" due process—which means the government must follow fair legal procedures when it punishes you or takes things from you. But *Griswold* involved what's known as "substantive" due process. Substantive due process centers on the word "liberty" in the amendment; it asks whether there are any fundamental rights the government cannot take away from you because doing so would deprive

A pro-choice march in 1977 in New York City

you of your liberty. In *Griswold*, the Supreme Court said privacy is one such right. In that way, the due process clause came to be the part of the Constitution that protected reproductive rights.

In 1972, the Supreme Court extended the right to contraception protected by *Griswold* to unmarried people. And in 1973, the Supreme Court built on this line of cases in *Roe v. Wade*. At the time, abortion was illegal in Texas. Jane Roe (a fake name used to protect her identity) brought a lawsuit challenging the Texas law, arguing that it violated her Fourteenth Amendment rights. The Supreme Court ruled in Roe's favor, holding that the right of privacy includes the right to make decisions for oneself—including the decision to end a pregnancy.

For almost fifty years after *Roe* was decided, the Constitution protected the right to abortion, and numerous state laws were struck down under the Fourteenth Amendment.

However, as time went on, the constitutional protections that *Roe* promised were eroded by the courts. Abortion became more and more political, with Republican states passing increasingly restrictive laws, and Republican-nominated judges repeatedly upholding them. In 1992's *Planned Parenthood v. Casey*, the Supreme Court held that abortion restrictions were unconstitutional only if they placed an "undue burden" on an individual's ability to access abortion. What it meant for a burden to be "undue" was vague, and lower courts were able to take advantage of that vagueness to uphold more and more restrictions. Over the years, the right protected by *Roe* slowly dwindled.

REPRODUCTIVE JUSTICE VERSUS REPRODUCTIVE RIGHTS

Historically, the mainstream reproductive rights movement has been led by wealthy, white, cis women who have focused on keeping abortion legal. By focusing only on legality, these advocates have failed to consider the factors that can make it impossible for people to access abortion even when it is legal—things like not being able to afford the procedure, take time off of work, or find childcare. Because of the way systemic racism works, these economic burdens fall disproportionately on people of color, and on Black people in particular.

In response to the gaps in the mainstream reproductive rights movement, Indigenous women, women of color, and trans people developed a different framework: reproductive justice. As the reproductive justice group SisterSong explains, reproductive justice is "the human right to maintain personal bodily autonomy, have children, not have children, and parent the children we have in safe and sustainable communities." Reproductive justice means fighting for abortion access, not just the right to abortion. It also means fighting for more than just abortion, like access to contraception, comprehensive sex education, prenatal and pregnancy care, domestic violence services, and adequate wages.

Whatever was left of *Roe* was eliminated altogether in 2022, when the Supreme Court decided *Dobbs v. Jackson Women's Health Organization*. In *Dobbs*, the Supreme Court considered whether a Mississippi law that banned abortion after fifteen weeks of pregnancy violated the Fourteenth Amendment. The court upheld the law and overruled *Roe*, holding that the right to abortion was not "fundamental" and so not protected by the due process clause. In other words: Abortion was no longer a constitutional right.

But just two years prior, in *June Medical Services v. Russo*, the Supreme Court had struck down a Louisiana abortion restriction and made clear that *Roe* was still the law of the land. The only thing that changed between *June Medical Services* and *Dobbs* was the composition of the court: Justice Ginsburg had passed away and was replaced by a conservative justice. As we've seen numerous times throughout this book, the outcome in *Dobbs* shows us that what the Constitution means is not set in stone. It is determined by the nine justices sitting on the bench, who may be influenced by their own agendas and ideals.

There is still much to do to achieve gender equality in the United States, and the Fourteenth Amendment is probably not going to be the answer.

Without *Roe*, the fight for reproductive rights and justice will need to look outside the courts. Reproductive justice organizations like SisterSong, for example, are working to change dialogue about abortion in the public sphere and to increase access to contraception, comprehensive sex education, and prenatal and pregnancy care, and organizations like the National Network of Abortion Funds are helping people who face financial barriers access abortion.

And while the equal protection clause initially proved useful in the fight for trans rights, that began to change in 2023, and may be completely undermined in the coming Supreme Court term. Organizations like the National Center for Transgender Equality are working for change outside the Supreme Court, advocating for policies that support the trans community and helping trans people navigate complicated name and gender change processes.

In the next chapter we'll see a similar story unfold in the realm of immigration. As with gender, the Fourteenth Amendment plays a part in the history of the fight for immigrants' rights, but it cannot be the solution to many of today's problems.

The Fight for Immigrants' Rights

In 1848, gold was discovered in California, triggering a period known as the Gold Rush. Hundreds of thousands of Americans flocked westward in the hope that they might get rich quick. While most of these Americans were white, "more than 2,000 African Americans traveled to California by 1852."

Others traveled from Latin America and China to become gold miners; in 1852 alone, more than twenty thousand Chinese people immigrated to California. Chinese immigrants also settled in mining towns in North and South Dakota.

As Chinese immigration increased, so too did anti-Chinese racism. Eventually, Congress would pass several anti-Chinese laws that were challenged under the Fourteenth Amendment. These cases still define the meaning of the amendment today.

While this chapter is not a comprehensive analysis of immigration law and policy, it will cover several important intersections of immigration with the Fourteenth Amendment, from laws that excluded Chinese immigrants during the Gold Rush, to laws that took away people's citizenship in the 1900s, to the forced relocation of Japanese people to prison camps during World War II. The principles from all these cases remain relevant and show us that the

Fourteenth Amendment has been more disappointing than helpful when it comes to the fight for immigrants' rights.

Chae Chan Ping and the Plenary Power Doctrine

After the Gold Rush died down, economic decline led to increased racial tensions. White Americans believed they were competing with Chinese immigrants for jobs to which they felt entitled; some businesses were even boycotted for employing Chinese people. (We still hear this argument about immigrants "taking jobs" from "real" Americans today.)

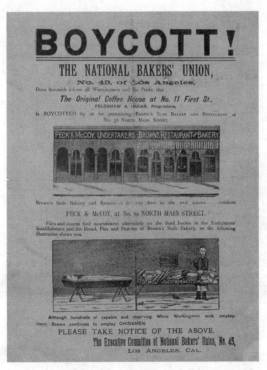

A flyer calling for the boycott of a Los Angeles bakery because it employed Chinese people instead of "capable and deserving White Workingmen"

Anti-Chinese racism led to the Chinese Massacre of 1871, in which a mob of five hundred white people descended on Los Angeles's Chinatown and lynched eighteen people, a tenth of the city's Chinese residents. Six years later, in 1877, another mob of white people attacked San Francisco's Chinatown, murdering four Chinese residents and destroying extensive property. The *San Francisco Chronicle* reported that "every Chinese house had evidently been carefully listed beforehand, for on the whole line of march and on either side of the streets there was not left a single one which was not utterly and completely sacked."

Los Angeles's Chinatown in 1880

Five years later, in 1882, Congress passed the first significant immigration law: the Chinese Exclusion Act, which would remain in effect until 1943. The act was both classist and racist. It banned Chinese laborers, defined as "skilled and unskilled laborers and

Chinese employed in mining," from immigrating into the United States, but Chinese merchants, teachers, students, and diplomats were still able to immigrate. As one scholar explains: "The Chinese Exclusion Act worked. In 1882, before it took effect, over 39,000 Chinese came to America. In 1887, Chinese immigration bottomed out at ten!"

In 1888, Congress passed an addendum to the Exclusion Act called the Scott Act, which said that any "Chinese laborer" who left the United States was not allowed to return.

The Supreme Court considered whether the Scott Act violated the Fourteenth Amendment in *Chae Chan Ping v. United States.* Plaintiff Chae Chan Ping was a Chinese subject who lived in San Francisco. He had immigrated to the United States to work as a laborer in 1875, before the Chinese Exclusion Act was passed. More than a decade later, he left the United States to visit China, which at that time he was allowed to do—he even obtained a re-entry certificate that said he was legally allowed to return to the United States. While he was sailing back, however, Congress passed the Scott Act, and when he arrived in San Francisco, he was turned away by customs officers.

Chae Chan Ping sued over his exclusion, arguing that his re-entry certificate gave him the right to return and that his right was taken away without any due process. The Fourteenth Amendment says that no state shall "deprive any person of life, liberty, or property, without due process of law; nor deny to any person within its jurisdiction the equal protection of the laws." Person, not citizen. Unlike the Fourteenth Amendment's privileges or immunities clause (which we discussed in chapters 3 and 4), the due process clause applies to *all* people in the United States—regardless of whether they are citizens.

The Supreme Court ruled against Chae Chan Ping and upheld the Scott Act. The court went beyond the reentry certificate issue, explaining that immigration concerned national security and so Congress's ability to regulate it was not "open to controversy." Using racist language about "foreigners of a different race" being "dangerous" and unable to "assimilate" (blend in), the court wrote:

> *If, therefore, the government of the United States, through its legislative department, considers the presence of foreigners of a different race in this country, who will not assimilate with us, to be dangerous to its peace and security, their exclusion is not to be stayed because at the time there are no actual hostilities with the nation of which the foreigners are subjects.*

Even though there was no conflict with China at the time, the court emphasized that there *could* be, and so Congress needed to be able to regulate immigration without being second-guessed by courts. In this way, the Supreme Court's opinion in *Chae Chan Ping v. United States* gave Congress and the executive branch the power to make decisions on immigration without courts acting as a check on that power—what's sometimes called the plenary power doctrine.

To this day, the plenary power doctrine defines immigration law. What it means is that while noncitizens may technically have a right to due process, this does not always hold up in practice. For example, immigration officials can stop and search anyone within a hundred miles of the U.S. border, even if they have no reason to suspect them of a crime. (Typically, the police must have a reason to stop and search you.) Noncitizens are not guaranteed lawyers in their immigration court proceedings, and those who have been convicted of crimes must be imprisoned while their immigration case moves forward. Because of the plenary power doctrine, which gives Congress broad leeway in regulating immigration, courts have not considered any of this to violate noncitizens' due process rights. "In immigration court, you have very few rights," says one attorney.

MEXICAN REPATRIATION

Starting in the late 1800s, U.S. employers recruited Mexican workers to build railroads and harvest crops. The demand for Mexican labor only increased after Congress passed laws restricting immigration from China, Japan, and Southern and Eastern Europe; between 1920 and 1930, a million Mexican people came to the United States for work.

The tide turned during the Great Depression, when the number of available jobs plummeted. Mexican workers were treated like scapegoats for "taking jobs away" from "real" Americans—an argument that was used against Chinese immigrants and that we still hear today. In 1931, the Los Angeles Chamber of Commerce noted that the slogan "Employ no Mexican while a white man is unemployed" had rapidly spread among the city's employers.

Los Angeles County (and later the federal government) launched a deportation campaign it called "repatriation." Sometimes this meant forcible deportation; other times private citizens intimidated Mexicans into leaving; still other times Mexicans left because they were barred from most jobs. No one is quite sure how many people of Mexican descent (many of them U.S. citizens) were forced to leave the United States during the Great Depression. Some historians say it was 350,000; others say more than one million.

The same cycle started all over again in 1941. With many American men fighting in World War II, U.S. employers brought millions of contract workers in from Mexico. In the mid-1950s, the tide turned: The U.S. government once again said that Mexican people were "taking jobs" from United States citizens, committing crimes, and taking advantage of public services. Much like today, this treatment was rationalized by refusing to see Mexican immigrants as humans—instead using hateful terms like "illegals" or "aliens." (Recall how similar methods were used to justify slavery.)

Once again, the federal government targeted numerous U.S. cities, deporting hundreds of thousands of Mexican immigrants and frightening many others into leaving. Approximately 1.5 million U.S. residents of Mexican descent left the country during the first half of the 1950s.

The term "repatriation" means sending someone back to their home country, implying that everyone forced out of the United States during these periods was a Mexican citizen. But numerous U.S. citizens of Mexican ancestry were forced out of the country; "they cannot be said to have been repatriated," one legal scholar writes.

Repatriation violated the constitutional rights of both citizens and noncitizens: U.S. citizens cannot be deported, and while "noncitizens may be subject to removal from the United States, due process generally protects all noncitizens in the country before they can be removed." Noncitizens were entitled to certain court proceedings, which they were not given.

Even though repatriation was of "questionable legality," it was not challenged, as "resistance was futile to the massive tide of anti-immigrant, anti-Mexican sentiment." Here, and as we'll see throughout this chapter, fear of immigrants was used to justify dehumanizing and racist policies, regardless of what the Constitution supposedly guaranteed.

Wong Kim Ark and Birthright Citizenship

In 1898's *United States v. Wong Kim Ark*, the Supreme Court considered whether a person of Chinese origin born in the United States was a U.S. citizen.

Wong Kim Ark was born in San Francisco around 1870 to parents who were Chinese subjects. In 1890, Wong visited China, then returned to the United States. But when he took another trip to China five years later and attempted to return, he was turned away at the border. Citing the Chinese Exclusion Act, which prevented people from China from entering the United States, immigration officials refused to let Wong come home. They didn't care that he'd been born in the United States; he was Chinese, and to them that was the end of the story.

Wong challenged his exclusion from the United States in a lawsuit that made its way to the Supreme Court. He argued that he was a U.S. citizen under the

Wong Kim Ark

Fourteenth Amendment's birthright citizenship clause—which says that "all persons born or naturalized in the United States, and subject to the jurisdiction thereof, are citizens of the United States and of the State wherein they reside"—and so should be allowed to return home.

It seemed pretty clear from the text of the Fourteenth Amendment that Wong had a winning argument. While the birthright citizenship clause was initially intended to grant citizenship upon Black people after the Civil War, it makes no explicit mention of race and should have applied to Wong, too. In fact, during debates on the amendment, congressmen explicitly said that Chinese immigrants' children would be citizens through the Fourteenth Amendment.

The government's attorneys fought against this interpretation in Wong's case, however, because they wanted to keep enforcing their racist laws. If a Chinese person could be a U.S. citizen, that meant that "the acts of Congress . . . prohibiting persons of the Chinese race, and especially Chinese laborers, from coming into the United States, do not and cannot apply to him." The government's attorneys argued that a "mere accident of birth"—the fact that Wong happened to be born in the United States—was an unacceptable loophole in the law.

To get around the most obvious reading of the amendment, the government's attorneys focused on the phrase "subject to the jurisdiction," the birthright citizenship clause's only exception: "all persons born or naturalized in the United States, *and subject to the jurisdiction thereof,* are citizens of the United States and of the State wherein they reside" (italics added). ("Subject to the jurisdiction" just means "subject to the laws" of a particular place.) The government's attorneys argued that Wong and other U.S.-born children of noncitizens were subject to *foreign* jurisdictions and so ineligible for birthright citizenship under the Fourteenth Amendment.

But this was not what Congress meant by this exception. As law professors Akhil Reed Amar and John C. Harrison explain, the "subject to the jurisdiction" clause was intended to apply to only two groups: Indigenous people, who had their own tribal governments, and the children of foreign diplomats "because under international law diplomats and their families were largely immune from the legal control and the courts of their host country." (Today, Indigenous people are U.S. citizens under the Indian Citizenship Act of 1924.) If the Supreme Court ruled against Wong, the clause would be much broader: Any person born in the United States whose parents were immigrants would lose their citizenship.

Wong's lawyers emphasized just how broad this interpretation was, explaining that it would also harm the children of white immigrants. Siding with Wong, the Supreme Court held that because Wong was born in the United States, he was a U.S. citizen under the citizenship clause of the Fourteenth Amendment. Just as Wong's lawyers had suspected, the court was unwilling to rule in such a way that even white citizens would be harmed: "To hold that the Fourteenth Amendment of the Constitution excludes from citizenship the children, born in the United States, of citizens or subjects of other countries," the court explained, "would be to deny citizenship to thousands of persons of English, Scotch, Irish, German or other European parentage, who have always been considered and treated as citizens of the United States."

The two dissenters in *Wong*—justices who disagreed with the majority—argued in their opinion that because Wong's parents were immigrants, Wong was not a citizen. They also used racist language, describing Chinese people as "strangers in the land" who, "unfamiliar with our institutions, and apparently incapable of assimilating with our people, might endanger good order, and be injurious to the public interests." This sort of hateful language reflects a fear of immigrants that reappears in Supreme Court opinions throughout American history.

The dissenters in *Wong* included Justice John Marshall Harlan, who had come out strongly against racial segregation just two years earlier in his dissent in *Plessy v. Ferguson* (which we discussed in chapter 7). There, Justice Harlan wrote: "We boast of the freedom enjoyed by our people above all other peoples. But it is difficult to reconcile that boast with a state of the law which, practically, puts the brand of servitude and degradation upon a large class of our fellow citizens, our equals before the law." In *Wong*, however, Justice Harlan adopted harmful stereotypes about Chinese people—degrading "a large class" of his "fellow citizens," who in his own words should have been his "equals before the law." Much like Susan B. Anthony, Justice Harlan adhered to some progressive ideals but ignored others.

In practical terms, the *Wong Kim Ark* ruling was not very helpful to Chinese people. To claim birthright citizenship, a Chinese person would have to produce two white witnesses who could swear to the truth of their statements, which was very hard for many Chinese people to do because of anti-Chinese racism. What's more, Chinese people were often arrested and forced to prove their citizenship—indeed, Wong himself was arrested in Texas in 1901 for being a "Chinese person" living "illegally" in the United States.

BIRTHRIGHT CITIZENSHIP TODAY

During his presidency, Donald Trump called for revocation of birthright citizenship, attempting to revive the argument the Supreme Court had rejected so many years prior in *Wong Kim Ark*. He wasn't the first to do so: Congress had tried to do the same in 1995 and 2005.

President Trump's focus was on "anchor babies," an offensive term for citizen children of noncitizen parents, often applied to people from Mexico. He argued that these children were not "subject to the jurisdiction" of the United States because their parents were not citizens—repeating the argument the government's lawyers had raised in *Wong Kim Ark*. While President Trump's attempt failed, the push to end birthright citizenship persists among conservatives and will likely be raised again under another administration.

Denaturalization

Once a citizen, always a citizen. Right?

Not really. Throughout American history, millions of people have been stripped of their U.S. citizenship—a process known as "denaturalization"—whether that's because of who they choose to marry, because of their political beliefs, or because they made an error in their naturalization papers.

In 1907, Congress passed the Expatriation Act, a federal law that revoked citizenship for women who married noncitizens. This law was based on the principles of "coverture" we discussed in the chapter on gender—that married women were "covered" by their husbands and weren't legal people separate from them. So if a woman who was a U.S. citizen married a man who was not, she took on his "foreign" identity. The Expatriation Act was also based on xenophobia (fear of outsiders), but a sexist form of it: American purity was tainted only if women were marrying foreign men, not the other way around. (Recall the similar panic surrounding white women's purity discussed in chapter 4.)

In 1915's *Mackenzie v. Hare*, a woman named Ethel Coope Mackenzie sought to challenge the 1907 law. She had lost her citizenship after marrying a noncitizen, Scottish singer Gordon Mackenzie. Ethel Mackenzie argued that the Expatriation Act violated the Fourteenth Amendment because all persons born in the United

States were citizens and Congress had no authority to take citizenship away.

She lost 9–0. The Supreme Court said that in marriage a husband and wife's identities merged and that the Expatriation Act was constitutional because marriage was voluntary and Mackenzie had notice of the consequences. Though this ruling may seem limited, it actually gave Congress a lot of power to take away people's citizenship. The ruling meant that, in theory, a law could revoke the citizenship of people who choose to live abroad, because living abroad is "voluntary" and they would have had "notice of the consequences."

And indeed, throughout the twentieth century, the U.S. government revoked citizenship as a political tool. In 1942, for example, the attorney general began a campaign to denaturalize people affiliated with certain political groups that the government considered radical or dangerous, including communists. After World War II, as tensions between the United States and the communist Soviet Union grew into the Cold War, Congress allowed denaturalization of people who participated in any "subversive activities" (activities that secretly undermine the government). This led to increased hysteria about whether people in the United States were loyal to their government or were secret communist sympathizers.

Numerous journalists and labor leaders were denaturalized on this basis, and countless others were intimidated into silence. Altogether, citizenship was treated like a privilege that the government could take away as it pleased. By the end of the twentieth century, writes law professor Amanda Frost, the U.S. government had denaturalized more people "than any other democracy before or since."

In 1967's *Afroyim v. Rusk*, the Supreme Court finally put some limits on the government's ability to denaturalize citizens. The court held that the Fourteenth Amendment guaranteed citizens the constitutional right to remain citizens; they couldn't be denaturalized for their speech, conduct, or politics:

> *"All persons born or naturalized in the United States . . . are citizens of the United States . . ." There is no indication in these words of a fleeting citizenship, good at the moment it is acquired but subject to destruction by the Government at any time. Rather the Amendment can most reasonably be read as defining a citizenship which a citizen keeps unless he voluntarily relinquishes it. Once acquired, this Fourteenth Amendment citizenship was not to be shifted, canceled, or diluted at the will of the Federal Government, the States, or any other governmental unit.*

Afroyim pumped the brakes on the government's rampant denaturalization: In the fifty years that followed, fewer than 150 people were denaturalized. But denaturalization took center stage again with Operation Janus and Operation Second Look.

Operation Janus started under President Barack Obama to identify naturalization fraud by looking at fingerprint data. With the addition of Operation Second Look under President Donald Trump, the program was greatly expanded into a mass denaturalization campaign that appeared to target people from Muslim majority countries. The campaign required government agencies to review records of naturalized citizens and begin denaturalization if there was any fraud or error in the naturalization process.

But what does it mean to commit fraud or make an error? Naturalization forms are incredibly long, and they include questions like "Have you EVER been arrested, cited, or detained by any law enforcement officer (including any immigration official or any official of the U.S. armed forces) for any reason?" You can only check yes or no, but such questions are open to interpretation. It's easy to make a small error that might later be viewed as fraud, and which could lead to the loss of citizenship. All of this is constitutional because *Afroyim* left an important exception: The government may still denaturalize citizens who committed fraud or error during the naturalization process.

RESTORING CITIZENSHIP TO CONFEDERATES

While numerous immigrants were being denaturalized, one group of people were getting their citizenship back: Confederates.

After the Civil War, Confederates were arguably no longer citizens of the United States; in claiming that they had started a new country, they had effectively expatriated themselves. But in 1865, President Andrew Johnson (remember him from chapter 2?) issued a proclamation that said most Confederates could reclaim citizenship if they took an oath to support the Constitution and the Union. Confederate leaders and wealthy property owners would have to ask Johnson for a pardon directly to regain their citizenship, which Johnson readily provided.

The restoration of Confederates' citizenship wasn't just confined to the 1800s. More than a century after the war, in 1975, Congress restored the citizenship of Robert E. Lee, the commander of the Confederate army. Congress called him a "patriotic citizen" even though he had, quite literally, waged war on the United States. Just three years later, in 1978, Jefferson

Davis, the president of the Confederacy, also had his citizenship restored.

While restoring citizenship to people who directly attacked the Union, the U.S. government was denaturalizing people whose mere ideas, or mere presence on U.S. soil, seemed to threaten its hold on power.

Korematsu and World War II

In World War II, the United States fought against Germany, Italy, and Japan. But immigrants from these countries were treated very differently: While Japanese Americans were forced to abandon their homes and relocate to prison camps simply because they were Japanese, German and Italian immigrants accused of being disloyal were treated as individuals. The sharply different ways immigrants from these countries were treated reveals the racism that motivated the government's actions.

In 1942, President Franklin Roosevelt issued Executive Order 9066, which allowed the secretary of war and military commanders "to prescribe military areas . . . from which any or all persons may be excluded" in order to preserve national security. While the order did not mention race explicitly, it led to the incarceration of an estimated 122,000 Japanese Americans in makeshift camps across the West and in Arkansas. With only a few days' or weeks' notice, Japanese people—over half of them citizens—were forced to leave their homes and jobs on the West Coast and sell or abandon their possessions.

The conditions in the camps were bleak. Many were located in harsh climates, where summers were hot and the winters were freezing; at one camp in Wyoming, winter temperatures fell to 30 degrees below zero. Rooms were overcrowded and disease spread rapidly. In a 1943 letter to President Roosevelt, the secretary of the interior wrote that "the situation in at least some of the Japanese internment camps is bad and is becoming worse rapidly."

Some Japanese American people refused to obey the government's orders, including a man named Fred Korematsu. Korematsu was

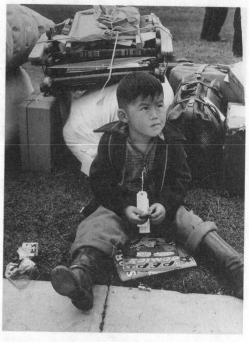

A 1942 photo of a child being evacuated, wearing what was known as an evacuation tag, a symbol of the internees' inhuman treatment

born in Oakland, California, in 1919 to parents who had emigrated from Japan to the United States, where they owned a flower nursery. On May 30, 1942, Korematsu was arrested in San Leandro, California, on "suspicion of being Japanese." He was sent to the Tanforan Assembly Center, a camp built on the grounds of a racetrack near San Francisco. There he had to live "in a horse stall with a cot, a straw mattress and one light bulb hanging down."

Korematsu decided to sue the government, arguing that Executive Order 9066 was unconstitutional. In *Korematsu v. United States*—a decision now considered one of the court's worst— the Supreme Court ruled 6–3 against him. The court held that Executive Order 9066 was necessary for national security and that Korematsu was not relocated "because of hostility to him or his race," but "because we are at war with the Japanese Empire."

In his dissent, Justice Frank Murphy highlighted the majority's hypocrisy: The United States was also at war with Germany and Italy, but only Japanese Americans were forced to relocate to prison camps. German and Italian Americans who were suspected of disloyal behavior were instead treated as individuals and allowed to explain their actions at hearings. This was "a level of individualized due process that was denied to the incarcerated Japanese Americans," law professor Amanda Frost explains. "In fact," writes journalist and historian Richard Reeves, "there was not a single American of Japanese descent, alien or citizen, charged with espionage or sabotage during the war. These men, women, and children were locked up for the duration of the war because they looked like the enemy, the troops of Imperial Japan, a place most of them had never seen."

A camp in Arcadia, California, where Japanese people were incarcerated

Because the relocation order was targeted at Japanese Americans, Justice Murphy explained in his dissent, it was "obvious racial discrimination" that deprived Japanese Americans "of the equal protection of the laws." And because it also "deprive[d] these individuals of their constitutional rights to live and work where they will, to establish a home where they choose and to move about freely," all "without benefit of hearings," it likewise violated their constitutional right to due process. He concluded, "I dissent, therefore, from this legalization of racism."

NONCITIZENS AND THE EQUAL PROTECTION CLAUSE

In 1886, the Supreme Court held that the equal protection clause protects both noncitizens and citizens in *Yick Wo v. Hopkins*. Plaintiff Yick Wo argued that while a San Francisco law targeting laundromats may have seemed impartial, it was actually targeted at Chinese Americans, who operated most laundromats in the city. The Supreme Court ruled in his favor and held that the law violated the equal protection clause. As the court explained, noncitizens were also granted equal protection rights by the Fourteenth Amendment.

Since then, the Supreme Court has ruled that the equal protection clause guarantees noncitizens equal access to welfare benefits, scholarships, and public schools, among other things. But whether these rights exist and whether people can actually take advantage of them are different stories. For many undocumented people, fear of deportation means that it can be too risky to assert any of these rights, despite being legally entitled to them. As with school desegregation after *Brown v. Board of Education*, there is a gap between what the law says and what rights people actually have in practice.

Korematsu shows us that injustice is often legal. The Supreme Court ruled that sending Japanese Americans to prison camps for years, forcing them to abandon their homes and jobs—simply because they were Japanese—was perfectly constitutional. As Justice Murphy noted in his dissent, the irony of these camps was profound: The United States was at war with Germany, which was sending millions of Jews, Roma, people with disabilities, and other targeted groups to concentration camps where they were murdered. The U.S. government's logic, Justice Murphy explained, "has been used in support of the abhorrent and despicable treatment of minority groups by the dictatorial tyrannies which this nation is now pledged to destroy." As the court made clear in *Korematsu*, the Constitution may not protect us from even the gravest injustices.

Korematsu was not overturned until 2018, in the case of *Trump v. Hawaii*. In that case, the Supreme Court considered whether President Trump's executive order banning immigration from a number of Muslim-majority countries violated the Constitution. Even though President Trump's public statements about the law made clear that it was intended to be a Muslim ban, the Supreme Court held that the law did not explicitly target people based on their religion. It was simply a list of countries, and they just happened to be majority Muslim.

The Supreme Court's opinion overruled *Korematsu*, explaining that "*Korematsu* has nothing to do with this case. The forcible relocation of U.S. citizens to concentration camps, solely and explicitly on the basis of race, is objectively unlawful and outside the scope of Presidential authority." But as the dissenters pointed out, the two cases were actually quite similar: In *Korematsu v. United States*, the court said it wasn't targeting Korematsu based on his race; the U.S. was just at war with Japan. In *Trump v. Hawaii*, the court said it wasn't targeting countries because they were majority Muslim; those countries just happened to pose national security risks. But in both cases, the anti-Japanese and Islamophobic motivations are obvious. In this way, the logic of *Korematsu* persists to this day.

Although the rights in the Fourteenth Amendment do not depend on citizenship, their value is still limited. Under the plenary power doctrine, Congress is able to trample on the due process rights of noncitizens. The push to end birthright citizenship continues, and where equal protection rights exist, their actual impact is limited.

The solutions to today's immigration problems are thus unlikely to be found in the Fourteenth Amendment. Across the country, organizations are working to effect change by other means: Make the Road New York, for example, focuses on policy change and community organizing; in Chicago, Organized Communities Against Deportations is "an undocumented-led group whose mission is to organize against the deportation, detention, criminalization, and incarceration of black, brown, and immigrant communities"; and the California Immigrant Policy Center "combines policy advocacy, strategic communications, statewide organizing, and regional coalition capacity building" to advocate for policies that protect immigrants and their families.

In the next chapter, we'll see a similar story about the limits of the Fourteenth Amendment play out in the fight for LGBTQ+ rights.

The Fight for LGBTQ+ Rights

Michael Hardwick was born in Miami in 1954. His family described him as kind and sensitive—he was always aware of how other people were feeling. After college, Hardwick moved to Atlanta, where he worked as a bartender at a gay bar called Cove.

One day in July 1982, Hardwick stepped out of the front door of Cove and threw a beer bottle in the trash can. Immediately, a police officer walked up to him and gave him a ticket for drinking alcohol in public. But Hardwick wasn't drinking—he was just cleaning up. The cop only ticketed him "because he knew I was gay," Hardwick later said.

That ticket would set into motion a court case over the Fourteenth Amendment and LGBTQ+ rights.

For many years, psychologists had labeled homosexuality a psychological disorder, stigmatizing LGBTQ+ people by labeling them as mentally ill. LGBTQ+ people were excluded from politics, "jury and military service, government jobs, professional licenses, and if foreign even entry into the United States." Queerness was—and still is—often seen as a threat to society because it disrupts the traditional family structure.

States also passed laws that banned sodomy, defined as oral or anal sex. Although heterosexual couples could also engage in such acts, these laws were targeted at LGBTQ+ people and served as "important state symbols that suggested shameful conduct." Sodomy laws made queerness a crime, and they meant that law enforcement officials could (and often did) blackmail people who they learned were gay.

Georgia's sodomy law was at the center of Michael Hardwick's case. Although there is a very long history of the fight for LGBTQ+ rights in the United States, this chapter will cover only its intersection with the Fourteenth Amendment—which begins in the 1980s with *Bowers v. Hardwick*.

DEFINING LGBTQ+

LGBTQ+ is an umbrella term that includes multiple identities: lesbian, gay, bisexual, transgender, and queer. Some of these terms concern sexual orientation (whom people are attracted to), while others refer to gender identity. These terms are defined by the Human Rights Campaign Foundation:

- **lesbian**: Women who are emotionally, romantically, or sexually attracted to other women. Women and nonbinary people may use this term to describe themselves.
- **gay**: People who are emotionally, romantically, or sexually attracted to members of the same gender. Men, women, and nonbinary people may use this term to describe themselves.
- **bisexual**: People who are emotionally, romantically, or sexually attracted to more than one sex, gender, or gender identity, though not necessarily simultaneously.
- **transgender** or **trans**: People whose gender identity or expression is different from cultural expectations based on the sex they were assigned at birth. The term does not imply a specific sexual orientation, and transgender people may identify as straight, gay, lesbian, bisexual, etc.

- **queer**: A term used to express a spectrum of identities and orientations that are counter to the mainstream. It is often used as a catchall to include many people, including those who do not identify as exclusively straight or who have nonbinary or gender-expansive identities. This term was previously used as a slur, but has been reclaimed by many people in the LGBTQ+ community.
- **+**: The plus sign recognizes the limitless sexual orientations and gender identities that exist.

Criminalizing Queerness

In the summer of 1982, the same police officer who ticketed Hardwick outside the gay bar entered his apartment to serve him with a warrant. The warrant was invalid because Hardwick had already paid the fifty-dollar fine, but the officer decided to serve it anyway.

The officer walked through Hardwick's apartment and into his

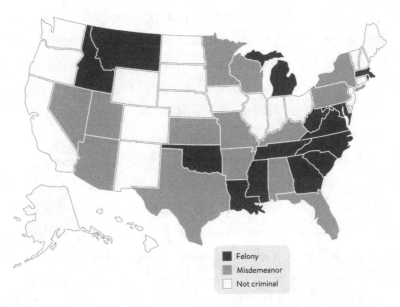

A map reflecting state laws regarding consensual sodomy in 1979

bedroom, where he saw Hardwick having consensual oral sex with another man. He arrested both men under a Georgia law that made sodomy a felony punishable by up to twenty years in prison. At the time, numerous other states had similar laws on the books.

The district attorney decided not to prosecute Hardwick because he thought the sodomy law shouldn't be applied to consensual sexual activity. But Hardwick knew that as a man who had sex with other men, he could always be prosecuted again by a different district attorney with a different opinion of the Georgia law.

Hardwick decided to sue the state, arguing that Georgia's sodomy law violated his right to privacy under the Fourteenth Amendment. He argued that laws making it a crime to engage in certain forms of consensual sexual activity deprive people of their liberty, which he believed should be considered part of the same privacy right the court recognized in *Griswold* and *Roe*.

In a split 5–4 opinion, the Supreme Court ruled against Hardwick and upheld the law's constitutionality, explaining that the Constitution does not confer "a fundamental right upon homosexuals to engage in sodomy." The chief justice in his concurring opinion quoted hateful language from two hundred years ago in describing homosexual sodomy as "the infamous crime against nature," an offense worse than rape, and "a crime not fit to be named."

But as the dissenters recognized, Hardwick's argument was broader than the way the majority characterized it: The case was not about "a fundamental right to engage in homosexual sodomy" but rather about "'the most comprehensive of rights and the right most valued by civilized men,' namely, 'the right to be let alone.'" The majority was purposefully viewing the issue as narrowly as possible—homosexual sodomy as opposed to privacy—so that it could say that no such right existed in the Constitution. The dissent concluded by explaining that "depriving individuals of the right to choose for themselves how to conduct their intimate relationships poses a far greater threat to the values most deeply rooted in our Nation's history than tolerance of nonconformity could ever do."

The decision appalled many LGBTQ+ people and their friends and allies. "It was a sign that the Court and, by extension, society did not accept homosexuals," writes one scholar. When the decision was issued, protests erupted in the streets of San Francisco, New York, and Washington D.C. More than a year later, people were still protesting: In October 1987, six hundred LGBTQ+ activists were arrested for trying to enter the Supreme Court "to approach the bench and to air their grievances before the Justices." *Bowers*, however, would remain the law of the land for nearly two decades.

In 2003, a nearly identical case reached the Supreme Court: *Lawrence v. Texas*. In that case, as in *Bowers*, two adult men—John Lawrence and Tyron Garner—were arrested for having consensual sex in private, this time under a Texas sodomy statute. The question before the Supreme Court was the same as in *Bowers*: Did the law violate the Fourteenth Amendment?

But this time, the Supreme Court struck down the law—explicitly overruling *Bowers*. The court explained that *Bowers* had been wrongly decided: "To say that the issue in *Bowers* was simply the right to engage in certain sexual conduct demeans the claim the individual put forward, just as it would demean a married couple were it said that marriage is simply about the right to have sexual intercourse."

Laws criminalizing private, consensual sex, the court concluded, violated the right to liberty in the Fourteenth Amendment's due process clause. The plaintiffs in the case were "entitled to respect for their private lives. The State cannot demean their existence or control their destiny by making their private sexual conduct a crime. Their right to liberty under the Due Process Clause gives them the full right to engage in their conduct without intervention of the government." For that reason, the court explained, "*Bowers* was not correct when it was decided, and it is not correct today. It ought not to remain binding precedent. *Bowers v. Hardwick* should be and now is overruled."

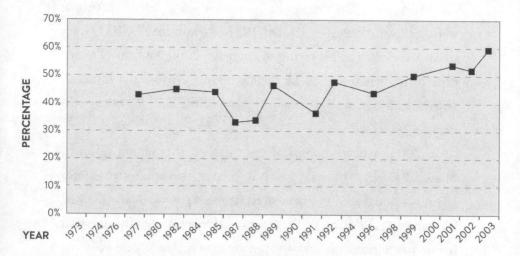

A graph showing changes in public opinion regarding whether "homosexual relations" should be legal, from 1973 to 2003

In the years between the two cases, public opinion had changed, as had the justices on the court. By the time *Lawrence* was decided in 2003, most Americans in a Gallup poll believed that "homosexual relations should be legal." Historians think this shift may have been caused by Americans having higher levels of education and more personal relationships with LGBTQ+ people, as well as by an increase in LGBTQ+ representation in television and media.

Historians also credit groups like the National LGBTQ Task

Force, which focused on repealing sodomy laws across the country after *Bowers* was decided. Working alongside historians, lawyers, and other LGBTQ+ organizations, the task force "was able to establish and expand the reach of statewide LGBT organizations, bring together gay and lesbian individuals, educate the public about gay rights issues, and put a 'human face' on the gay rights movement." Eventually, this work would help set the stage for the overruling of *Bowers* in *Lawrence v. Texas*.

Marriage Equality

In addition to decriminalization, some LGBTQ+ advocates began to fight for marriage equality. The campaign for marriage was "never a broad-based movement among gay and lesbian activists," writes Michael Warner in *The Trouble with Normal: Sex, Politics, and the Ethics of Queer Life*. To the contrary, many "early gay and lesbian rights advocates forged alliances with others who challenged the primacy of marriage," explains Nancy Polikoff, law professor and LGBTQ+ rights activist. Polikoff continues:

> *The gay rights movement was part of broader social movements challenging the political, economic, and social status quo and seeking to transform society into one in which sex, race, class, sexual orientation, and marital status no longer determined one's place in the nation's hierarchy. Marriage was in the process of losing its ironclad grip on the organization of family life, and lesbians and gay men benefited overwhelmingly from the prospect of a more pluralistic vision of relationships.*

As we saw in the chapter on gender, marriage can be an oppressive institution—one that fails to account for the various family and relationship structures in which LGBTQ+ people, and many other people, live. For many activists, write William N. Eskridge Jr. and Christopher R. Riano in *Marriage Equality: From Outlaws to In-Laws*, "gay liberation meant something more than equal treatment and expanded choice (such as the option to marry). It meant transformation of the status quo, not assimilation into it."

Not everyone agreed. For Mike McConnell and Jack Baker, two white men who started dating after they met at a Halloween party in Oklahoma City in 1966, marriage meant equality. "If other couples have the right to marry, so do we," McConnell told Baker after Baker suggested they move in together. "Well, I guess I'm going to have to figure out how we can do that, then," Baker replied.

When people think of marriage equality, they usually think of the 2015 Supreme Court case of *Obergefell v. Hodges*, in which the Supreme Court ruled that the Fourteenth Amendment protected the right to same-sex marriage. But decades earlier, McConnell and Baker had attempted to bring a very similar case.

In 1971, McConnell and Baker were denied a marriage license and decided to sue. They argued that nothing in the Minnesota statutes defined marriage as between a man and a woman and that they were unconstitutionally "deprived of liberty and property without due process" and "denied the equal protection of the laws, both guaranteed by the Fourteenth Amendment."

Their case eventually made its way to the Minnesota Supreme Court, which ruled against them. The court explained that "the institution of marriage as a union of man and woman, uniquely involving the procreation and rearing of children within a family, is as old as the book of Genesis." The court didn't buy the couple's argument that their case was like *Loving v. Virginia*, which said it was unconstitutional to ban interracial marriages. "There is a clear distinction between a marital restriction based merely upon race," the court explained, "and one based upon the fundamental difference in sex."

The couple asked the U.S. Supreme Court to review the Minnesota decision, but the justices refused to even hear their case because, they said, there was no "substantial federal question"—marriage was an issue that belonged to the states.

Baker and McConnell in 1970

Before the Minnesota Supreme Court was final, however, McConnell and Baker applied for a marriage license in a different Minnesota county—and obtained one because Baker had changed his legal name to Pat Lyn to be more gender neutral. Despite the courts' rulings, they were able to get married.

Marriage equality didn't reach the Supreme Court until 2013, in *United States v. Windsor.* In that case, the court considered whether the Defense of Marriage Act (DOMA)—which had been signed into law by President Bill Clinton in 1996—was constitutional.

DOMA defined marriage as between one man and one woman and said that states could refuse to acknowledge same-sex marriages that had been licensed by other states. Before signing the bill, President Clinton explained that while he opposed discrimination against gay people and encouraged Congress to pass a law preventing employers from discriminating against gay employees, he had also "long opposed governmental recognition of same-gender marriages."

A white woman named Edie Windsor brought a challenge to DOMA, arguing that marriage has benefits and tax breaks that she could not access as a gay person. While Windsor's marriage to her wife, Thea Spyer, had been recognized by the state of New York, DOMA prevented the federal government from recognizing it as well. This meant that when Spyer passed away and left Windsor an estate, Windsor had to pay substantial taxes because she did not qualify for the marital exception to federal estate tax. Windsor argued that this differential treatment violated her right to equal protection under the Fifth Amendment. (Remember from chapter 8 that when the challenged law is federal, it is the Fifth Amendment right to equal protection that applies.)

The Supreme Court ruled in Windsor's favor, striking down DOMA as a violation of equal protection because it "impose[d] a disadvantage, a separate status, and so a stigma upon all who enter into same-sex marriages." This didn't mean same-sex marriage was legal everywhere, though—just that the federal government had to

Edie Windsor after oral argument in her case before the Supreme Court

recognize same-sex marriages licensed in the states where they were legal.

Marriage finally became the law of the land in 2015's *Obergefell v. Hodges*. Jim Obergefell and his partner, John Arthur—both white men—wanted to get married, but they lived in Ohio, where same-sex marriage was banned. In 2011, Arthur was diagnosed with ALS, a disease that left him only a few years to live. After the court's *Windsor* ruling in 2013, the couple got married in Maryland, where same-sex marriage was legal. But they knew that if Arthur died in Ohio, his death record would say he was unmarried; Obergefell's name wouldn't be listed as the surviving spouse. For that reason, the couple brought a lawsuit challenging the Ohio ban.

Their case made it up to the Supreme Court, where it was combined with several other cases on the same issue. In a 5–4 opinion, the court held that the Fourteenth Amendment protected the right

Jim Obergefell exiting the Supreme Court after oral arguments in his case

of same-sex couples to marry. Writing for the majority, Justice Anthony Kennedy explained that the Fourteenth Amendment was a "charter" for liberty: While same-sex marriage wasn't specifically envisioned by the men who wrote the amendment, their concept of liberty was expansive enough to encompass it. The Constitution, he explained, granted people equal dignity through the Fourteenth Amendment.

In an often-quoted passage, the court wrote:

> *No union is more profound than marriage, for it embodies the highest ideals of love, fidelity, devotion, sacrifice, and family. In forming a marital union, two people become something greater than once they were. As some of the petitioners in these cases demonstrate, marriage*

embodies a love that may endure even past death. It would
misunderstand these men and women to say they disrespect
the idea of marriage. Their plea is that they do respect
it, respect it so deeply that they seek to find its fulfillment
for themselves. Their hope is not to be condemned to live
in loneliness, excluded from one of civilization's oldest
institutions. They ask for equal dignity in the eyes of the law.
The Constitution grants them that right.

Thinking Beyond Marriage

Not all supporters of LGBTQ+ rights celebrated the *Obergefell* decision. While equality was, of course, a good thing, some activists worried that the decision's focus on marriage might harm those LGBTQ+ people who chose not to marry. As law professor Melissa Murray explains in her essay, "*Obergefell v. Hodges* and Nonmarriage Inequality":

Although the Obergefell *decision is a victory for same-*
sex couples that wish to marry, it is likely to have negative
repercussions for those—gay or straight—who, by choice or
by circumstance, live their lives outside of marriage . . . By
further entrenching marriage's priority, Obergefell's *pro-*
marriage impulse not only demeans and challenges the status
of nonmarriage, it undermines the values and principles that
underlie the jurisprudence of nonmarriage. Thus, even as
Obergefell *expands the right to marry, it may also diminish*
constitutional protection for life outside of marriage.

In other words, Murray argues that by deeming marriage the most "profound" relationship people can have, *Obergefell* may have negative impacts on people who choose not to marry. As one example, unmarried couples (whether LGBTQ+ or straight) may find it more difficult to adopt children after *Obergefell*. Murray's argument echoed those of other scholars: For years, advocates had warned that the fight for marriage equality risked "reversing, rather than advancing, progress for diverse family forms," as Nancy Polikoff wrote in 2008.

Other critiques of *Obergefell* suggested that there were more urgent rights than marriage that should have been sought first. There were only so many resources to go around—whether that's attention from media outlets or money to spend on legal fees or funnel toward advocacy—and marriage, some LGBTQ+ activists believed, shouldn't have been the priority.

In his book *Normal Life: Administrative Violence, Critical Trans Politics, and the Limits of Law*, law professor Dean Spade explains that "the framing of marriage as the most essential legal need of queer people, and as the method through which queer people can obtain key benefits in many realms, ignores how race, class, ability, indigeneity, and immigration status determine access to those benefits," and so focuses only on "the most privileged gays and lesbians."

For trans people in particular, Spade continues, the most pressing issues include criminalization, immigration enforcement, lack of ID access, sex-segregated facilities, and lack of access to gender-affirming care. He argues that what might actually make a difference in the lives of trans people would be fighting to change the "rules that govern gender classification on ID, rules that govern sex-segregation of key institutions (shelters, group homes, jails, prisons, bathrooms), and rules that govern access to gender-confirming care for trans people"—not necessarily the right to marriage.

EMPLOYMENT DISCRIMINATION

As we learned in prior chapters, the Fourteenth Amendment has been interpreted so that it applies only to the actions of state governments, not private individuals. That means that private, nongovernmental employers who discriminate against their employees—whether based on their race, gender, or sexual orientation—can't be sued under the Fourteenth Amendment.

Instead, it's a law passed by Congress that provides employees with protection: the Civil Rights Act of 1964. Title VII of that act makes it unlawful for an employer to discriminate because of an "individual's race, color, religion, sex, or national origin." In 2020's *Bostock v. Clayton County*, the Supreme Court ruled that discrimination "because of . . . sex" in Title VII also includes discrimination on the basis of sexual orientation or transgender identity.

It is extremely hard, however, for plaintiffs to prevail in Title VII lawsuits. In federal courts between 1979 and 2006, plaintiffs in employment discrimination cases won only 15 percent of cases—compared to 51 percent of cases for plaintiffs in non-employment cases. Courts have held that it is not national origin discrimination to refuse to hire people with accents, for example, and that it is not race discrimination to fire people who wear hairstyles common in Black communities.

In *Normal Life*, Spade raises additional "questions about the usefulness of" antidiscrimination laws like Title VII. While such laws may have good intentions, he writes, they ignore the fact that most discrimination is systemic. Antidiscrimination laws assume power operates on an individual level—like an employer firing someone immediately after discovering they were gay. But as critical race theory teaches, systemic racism—like segregation in housing, or underfunding of primarily Black schools—is far more common than individual racism. For structural discrimination, laws like Title VII are often of little use.

In the years after he brought his case to the Supreme Court, Michael Hardwick worked as a scenic designer in Florida. He created large papier-mâché sculptures and installations for nightclubs—like a twelve-foot-long bright green lizard to be displayed over a bar. But what happened to him in Atlanta affected his personal relationships. In 1990, he explained that his case had a "chilling effect" on him and that he had not "had a steady relationship since then."

As it stands, the Fourteenth Amendment does not do nearly enough to protect LGBTQ+ people—but even those limited protections may soon disappear. As we saw in chapter 8, when the Supreme Court overturned *Roe* in *Dobbs*, it put into question whether other Fourteenth Amendment cases based on that same privacy right, like *Obergefell*, should be overturned. If that were to happen, marriage equality would no longer be protected by the Constitution.

As we've seen throughout this book, the next steps in the fight for LGBTQ+ rights likely exist outside the Fourteenth Amendment, and instead in community activism and reshaping public narratives. Organizations like GLAAD, as one example, use "entertainment, news, and digital media to share stories from the LGBTQ community that accelerate acceptance." Next steps may also include electing state and local officials who support LGBTQ+ rights, or even bringing cases in state courts under state laws or constitutions. For example, the New Jersey Department of Corrections in 2021 "agreed to adopt a system-wide policy to help protect transgender, intersex, and non-binary people in prisons" after the American Civil Liberties Union brought a lawsuit under a New Jersey civil rights law. While the Fourteenth Amendment may no longer be front and center, its spirit of equality persists in these other methods of fighting for LGBTQ+ rights.

Conclusion

The Fourteenth Amendment was the beginning of a long, non-linear march toward progress. There is still so much unfinished work: LGBTQ+ people still face discrimination based on their sexual orientation or gender identity; Black communities still experience violence and police brutality; access to reproductive health care, including abortion, is still extremely limited; immigrants still face deportation and denial of due process rights . . . the list goes on.

The story of the Fourteenth Amendment shows us the limits of law. Throughout this book, we've seen examples of how the composition of the Supreme Court has determined the outcome of a given case—how one court can make one decision and another court a few years later, composed of different people, can make the opposite decision. While this has sometimes happened in ways that support equality (like when *Brown* overruled *Plessy* or *Lawrence* overruled *Bowers*) it has also happened in the other direction (like when *Dobbs* overruled *Roe* or the Missouri Supreme Court changed course in *Dred Scott*). These changes show us that the law is not set in stone and that external forces often shape its meaning.

And even when the Supreme Court has ruled in ways that support equality, there is frequently a gap between what the law says and what rights people can actually take advantage of. We saw this in chapter 7, for example, when we discussed the aftermath of *Brown v. Board of Education*; in chapter 8, when we learned about reproductive justice and the difference between the right to abortion and abortion access; in chapter 9, when we saw the reality of Fourteenth Amendment rights for noncitizens; and in chapter 10, when learning about the limited usefulness of antidiscrimination laws in the workplace.

But more than that: Evil has so often been legal. Mass incarceration, police violence, segregated education and housing systems, voting rights restrictions, wealth inequality, life expectancy inequality—all of these are legal.

And in many of the horrible cases we've learned about—like *Plessy*, *Korematsu*, and *Dred Scott*—the Supreme Court didn't make any legal errors. The legal reasoning in these cases is perfectly sound, showing us that "what makes something constitutional is not its substantive justice but the ability of someone to justify it using constitutional vocabulary." Justice and constitutionality are not the same thing.

"In general, law school teaches people how to stop thinking outside of legal solutions to problems," Dean Spade explains, "which often means we can only think of ways to slightly tinker with harmful systems, thereby strengthening, stabilizing, and legitimizing them. The focus of legal education is working inside the existing legal system." James Ramsey, a law student in 2021, agrees: "There is a lurking tendency for lawyers, because of our conservative, risk-averse training, to quell radical thought and tactics—in the name of precedent and rationality—and instead bow to the law."

The solutions to many of today's problems might not have anything to do with the Fourteenth Amendment, or even with the law. Throughout this book, we've explored what that might look like: community activism, organizing, or working to change public narratives. There are also groups like Demand Justice organizing for

Supreme Court reform, who advocate for policies like term limits to help make the court more accountable.

In ways like these, we can continue to fight for the ideals of equality in the Fourteenth Amendment. We are all people of equal dignity, deserving of equal protection. Whether we strive for those goals in the courts or outside of them, the fight for a more equal nation is what must guide us.

Resources
to Learn More

"14th Amendment: Citizenship Rights, Equal Protection,
Apportionment, Civil War Debt," National Constitution Center
constitutioncenter.org/the-constitution/amendments/amendment-xiv

"Slavery in America: The Montgomery Slave Trade,"
Equal Justice Initiative
eji.org/reports/slavery-in-america

"The 1619 Project," *New York Times Magazine*
nytimes.com/interactive/2019/08/14/magazine/1619-america-slavery.html

Amend: The Fight for America,
created by Robe Imbriano, Tom Yellin
netflix.com/title/80219054

"14th Amendment to the U.S. Constitution: Primary
Documents in American History," Library of Congress
guides.loc.gov/14th-amendment

"From Dred Scott to the Civil Rights Act of 1875: Eighteen
Yers of Change," DocsTeach, created by the National Archives
docsteach.org/activities/teacher/from-dred-scott-to-the-civil-rights-act-of-
1875-eighteen-years-of-change

Selected Bibliography

Amar, Akhil Reed. *America's Constitution: A Biography*. New York: Random House, 2005.

Baer, Judith A. *Equality Under the Constitution: Reclaiming the Fourteenth Amendment*. Ithaca, NY: Cornell University Press, 1983.

Cheney, Charise. "Blacks on *Brown*: Intra-Community Debates over School Desegregation in Topeka, Kansas, 1941–1955." *Western Historical Quarterly* 42, no. 4 (Winter 2011).

Chin, Gabriel J. "*Chae Chan Ping* and *Fong Yue Ting*: The Origins of Plenary Power." In *Immigration Stories*, edited by David A. Martin and Peter H. Schuck. New York: Foundation Press, 2005.

Curtis, Michael Kent. *No State Shall Abridge: The Fourteenth Amendment and the Bill of Rights*. Durham, NC: Duke University Press, 1986.

Epps, Garrett. *Democracy Reborn: The Fourteenth Amendment and the Fight for Equal Rights in Post–Civil War America*. New York: Henry Holt, 2006.

Eskridge Jr., William N. *Dishonorable Passions: Sodomy Laws in America, 1861–2003*. New York: Viking, 2008.

Eskridge Jr., William N. and Christopher R. Riano. *Marriage Equality: From Outlaws to In-Laws*. Yale, CT: Yale University Press, 2020.

Finkelman, Paul. Dred Scott v. Sandford: *A Brief History with Documents*. 2nd ed. Boston: Bedford/St. Martin's, 2017.

Foner, Eric. *Fiery Trial: Abraham Lincoln and American Slavery*. New York: Norton, 2010.

———. *Reconstruction: America's Unfinished Revolution, 1863–1877*. 2nd ed. New York: Harper Perennial, 2014.

———. *The Second Founding: How the Civil War and Reconstruction Remade the Constitution*. New York: Norton, 2019.

Frost, Amanda. *You Are Not American: Citizenship Stripping from Dred Scott to the Dreamers*. Boston: Beacon Press, 2021.

Hannah-Jones, Nikole. "Our Democracy's Founding Ideals Were False When They Were Written. Black Americans Have Fought to Make Them True." *New York Times Magazine*, August 14, 2019.

Meyer, Howard N. *The Amendment That Refused to Die*. Radnor, PA: Chilton, 1973.

Murray, Melissa. "*Obergefell v. Hodges* and Nonmarriage Inequality." *California Law Review* 104, no. 5 (October 2016).

Polikoff, Nancy. *Beyond (Straight and Gay) Marriage*. Boston, MA: Beacon Press, 2008.

Rakove, Jack N. *Original Meanings: Politics and Ideas in the Making of the Constitution*. New York: Knopf, 1996.

Reeves, Richard. *Infamy: The Shocking Story of the Japanese American Internment in World War II*. New York: Henry Holt, 2015.

Root, Damon. *A Glorious Liberty: Frederick Douglass and the Fight for an Antislavery Constitution*. Lincoln: University of Nebraska Press, 2020.

Spade, Dean. *Normal Life: Administrative Violence, Critical Trans Politics, and the Limits of Law*. New York: South End Press, 2011.

Taylor, Alan. *American Revolutions: A Continental History, 1750–1804*. New York: Norton, 2016.

Wells, Ida B. *Southern Horrors: Lynch Law in All Its Phases*. New York: New York Age Print, 1892.

Wood, Gordon S. *American Revolution: A History*. New York: Modern Library, 2002.

Source Notes

Introduction

x "paramount destiny": *Bradwell v. The State*, 83 U.S. 130, 141 (1873) (Bradley, J., concurring).

x "Chinese person" living: Amanda Frost, *You Are Not American: Citizenship Stripping from Dred Scott to the Dreamers* (Boston: Beacon Press, 2021), 67.

Chapter 1

3 Most lawmakers at the time: Eric Foner, *The Second Founding: How the Civil War and Reconstruction Remade the Constitution* (New York: Norton, 2019), 17, 18, 31.

3 Madison, however, believed state governments: 1 Annals of Cong. 458 (1789).

5 Under the Articles, states were operating: Gordon S. Wood, *American Revolution: A History* (New York: Modern Library, 2002), 71–72.

5 "The long, hard war": Alan Taylor, *American Revolutions: A Continental History, 1750–1804* (New York: Norton, 2016), 361.

5 It needed "new powers": Taylor, *American Revolutions*, 372–73.

6 "No known black people": J. Clay Smith Jr., "Justice and Jurisprudence and the Black Lawyer," *Notre Dame Law Review* 69, no. 5 (March 2014): 1087.

6 "convinced him of the dangers": "James Madison and Executive Power," lesson plan, Center for Civic Education, 2001, www.civiced.org/lesson-plans /madison.

7 "scholarly, sickly": Taylor, *American Revolutions*, 371.

7 "weak of voice": *Encyclopedia Britannica*, s.v., "James Madison," by Irving Brant, last updated June 30, 2023, www.britannica.com/biography/James-Madison.

10 In 1787, Madison suggested: Akhil Reed Amar, *America's Constitution: A Biography* (New York: Random House, 2005), 320; see also Jack N. Rakove, *Original Meanings: Politics and Ideas in the Making of the Constitution* (New York: Knopf, 1996), 51.

10 "Another happy effect": James Madison to George Washington, April 16, 1787, Founders Online, National Archives, founders.archives.gov/documents /Madison/01-09-02-0208. (Madison's occasional ampersands have been changed to "and.")

11 They thought that a national veto: Rakove, *Original Meanings*, 51; see also Amar, *America's Constitution*, 320.

13 But many states were unhappy: Howard N. Meyer, *The Amendment That Refused to Die* (Radnor, PA: Chilton, 1973), 7–8; Taylor, *American Revolutions*, 387, 390.

18 "No State shall violate": "Senate Revisions to House Proposed Amendments to the U.S. Constitution," September 9, 1789, Records of U.S. Senate, 1789–2022, Record Group 46, National Archives, identifier 3535588, catalog .archives.gov/id/3535588?objectPage=3.

18 "If there was any reason to restrain": 1 Annals of Cong. 784 (1789).

18 So while the Lost Fourteenth: Rakove, *Original Meanings*, 335.

19 "I know, in some": 1 Annals of Cong. 458 (1789).

19 "If they are incorporated": 1 Annals of Cong. 457 (1789).

20 "the most valuable amendment": 1 Annals of Cong. 784 (1789).

20 "much better": 1 Annals of Cong. 783 (1789) (statement of Rep. Thomas Tudor Tucker of South Carolina).

20 to protect "state assemblies": Rakove, *Original Meanings*, 335.

20 The point of the Bill of Rights: Amar, *America's Constitution*, 320.

20 "The Senate have sent back": James Madison to Edmund Pendleton, September 14, 1789, Founders Online, National Archives, founders.archives .gov/documents/Madison/01-12-02-0258.

Chapter 2

23 "enslavers came from all parts": Julie Zauzmer Weil, Adrian Blanco, and Leo Dominguez, "More than 1,800 Congressmen Once Enslaved Black People. This Is Who They Were, and How They Shaped the Nation," *Washington Post*, January 10, 2022, https://www.washingtonpost.com/history/interactive/2022 /congress-slaveowners-names-list/.

24 By 1860, about 10 percent: Joseph C. G. Kennedy, comp., introduction to *Population of the United States in 1860 Compiled from the Original Returns of the Eighth Census* (Washington, D.C, 1864), x, xii.

24 Even for free Black people: Mary Elliott and Jazmine Hughes, "Four Hundred Years After Enslaved Africans Were First Brought to Virginia, Most Americans Still Don't Know the Full Story of Slavery," *New York Times Magazine*, August 19, 2019, www .nytimes.com/interactive/2019/08/19/magazine/history-slavery-smithsonian.html.

25 "I say it with a sad sense": Frederick Douglass, *Oration, Delivered in Corinthian Hall, Rochester, July 5th, 1852* (Rochester, NY, 1852), 15.

25 three main theories about the Constitution: Discussion of all three comes from Judith A. Baer, *Equality Under the Constitution: Reclaiming the Fourteenth Amendment* (Ithaca, NY: Cornell University Press, 1983), 59–60; and Foner, *Second Founding*, 9.

28 Frederick Douglass moved: Foner, *Second Founding*, 9.

28 "gradually and only after much brooding": Damon Root, *A Glorious Liberty: Frederick Douglass and the Fight for an Antislavery Constitution* (Lincoln: University of Nebraska Press, 2020), 2.

28 "Now, take the constitution": Douglass, *Oration*, 37.

29 the Missouri Supreme Court: *Winny v. Whitesides*, 1 Mo. 472 (1824).

29 "In the opinion of the court": *Dred Scott v. Sandford*, 60 U.S. 393, 407 (1857).

31 "It would give to persons": *Dred Scott*, 60 U.S. at 417.

32 "settle the slavery question": Paul Finkelman, Dred Scott v. Sandford: *A Brief History with Documents*, 2nd ed. (Boston: Bedford/St. Martin's, 2017), 38–39.

32 "wicked" and "abominable": Editorials, *New York Daily Tribune*, March 7 and 11, 1857.

33 Proslavery Democrats started using: David S. Reynolds, *John Brown, Abolitionist: The Man Who Killed Slavery, Sparked the Civil War, and Seeded Civil Rights* (New York: Knopf, 2005), 8.

33 "By the eve of the Civil War": Matthew Desmond, "In Order to Understand the Brutality of American Capitalism, You Have to Start on the Plantation," *New York Times Magazine*, August 14, 2019, www.nytimes.com /interactive/2019/08/14/magazine/slavery-capitalism.html.

33 "an increasing hostility": Declaration of the Immediate Causes Which Induce and Justify the Secession of South Carolina from the Federal Union, December 24, 1860, Avalon Project, Yale Law School, avalon.law.yale.edu/19th_century /csa_scarsec.asp.

33 "thoroughly identified with the institution": Declaration of the Immediate Causes Which Induce and Justify the Secession of the State of Mississippi from the Federal Union, [January 9, 1861], Avalon Project, Yale Law School, avalon .law.yale.edu/19th_century/csa_missec.asp.

34 "The North initially went to war": James W. Loewen, "Five Myths About Why the South Seceded," opinion, *Washington Post*, February 26, 2011, www.washingtonpost.com/outlook/five-myths-about-why-the-south -seceded/2011/01/03/ABHr6jD_story.html.

34 "If I could save the Union": Abraham Lincoln, letter to the editor, *New York Daily Tribune*, August 25, 1862.

34 "a physical difference": "Fourth Lincoln-Douglas Debate, Charleston, Illinois," September 18, 1858, in *Abraham Lincoln: Speeches and Writings 1832–1858*, ed. Don E. Fehrenbacher (New York: Library of America, 1989), 636; see also George M. Fredrickson, *Big Enough to Be Inconsistent: Abraham Lincoln Confronts Slavery and Race* (Cambridge, MA: Harvard University Press, 2008), 75.

34 "he never became": Foner, *Fiery Trial: Abraham Lincoln and American Slavery* (New York: Norton, 2010), xviii.

35 census data suggest: Guy Gugliotta, "New Estimate Raises Civil War Death Toll," *New York Times*, April 2, 2012, www.nytimes.com/2012/04/03/science /civil-war-toll-up-by-20-percent-in-new-estimate.html.

36 "Are we good enough": *Proceedings of the National Convention of Colored Men, Held in the City of Syracuse, N.Y., October 4, 5, 6, and 7; with the Bill of Wrongs and Rights, and the Address to the American People* (Boston, 1864), 58, African American Pamphlet Collection, Library of Congress, hdl.loc.gov/loc.rbc /rbaapc.20100.

36 "It is also unsatisfactory": Abraham Lincoln, "Last Public Address," April 11, 1865, in *American History Through Its Greatest Speeches: A Documentary History of the United States*, ed. Jolyon P. Girard, Darryl Mace, and Courtney Smith (Santa Barbara, CA: ABC-CLIO, 2017), vol. 2, 218.

37 "That is the last speech": Booth conspirator Payne (aka Lewis Powell) told this to Thomas T. Eckert, *Impeachment Investigation: Testimony Taken Before the Judiciary Committee of the House of Representatives in the Investigation of the Charges Against Andrew Johnson*, 39th Cong. 2nd Sess., 40th Cong. 1st Sess. (1867), 674, quoted in Girard, Mace, and Smith, *American History Through Speeches*, 216.

37 "This is a white man's country": "White Reconstruction," *National Anti-Slavery Standard*, September 16, 1865, quoted in "The Real Point at Issue," *Buffalo Daily Courier*, September 20, 1865.

37 Johnson came to oppose slavery: Sarah Fling, "The Formerly Enslaved Households of President Andrew Johnson," White House Historical Association, March 5, 2020, www.whitehousehistory.org/the-formerly -enslaved-households-of-president-andrew-johnson.

37 Johnson also thought: Aaron Astor, "When Andrew Johnson Freed His Slaves," Opinionater, *New York Times*, August 9, 2013, nyti.ms/3rC6Nql.

38 "seemingly unlimited authority": Foner, *Second Founding*, 31.

39 The Black codes effectively reestablished: Eric Foner, *Reconstruction: America's Unfinished Revolution, 1863–1877*, 2nd ed. (New York: Harper Perennial, 2014), 201.

39 "whole thought and time": Benjamin F. Flanders to Henry C. Warmoth, November 23, 1865, Henry Clay Warmoth Papers, 1798–1953, Southern Historical Collection, University of North Carolina, quoted in Foner, *Reconstruction*, 199.

39 "all persons born in the United States": Civil Rights Act of 1866, 14 Stat. 27 (1866).

39 Citizens, of every race and color: Civil Rights Act of 1866, 14 Stat. 27 (1866).

40 prison population skyrocketed . . . people imprisoned were Black: Foner, *Second Founding*, 50.

Chapter 3

44 Stevens had pushed for the joint committee: Baer, *Equality Under the Constitution*, 76; Meyer, *Amendment That Refused to Die*, 57–58.

44 Bingham's politics aligned: Gerard N. Magliocca, *American Founding Son: John Bingham and the Invention of the Fourteenth Amendment* (New York: NYU Press, 2013), 82–83.

45 The first issue tackled: Meyer, *Amendment That Refused to Die*, 54–55.

45 less than 2 percent: Kennedy, *Population of United States in 1860*, iv, vii, x.

46 In the Senate, the amendment was opposed: Foner, *Second Founding*, 63.

46 "most respectfully but earnestly pray": Cong. Globe, 39th Cong., 1st Sess. 848 (1866).

46 "The feeling in many portions of the country": Report of the Joint Committee on Reconstruction, 39th Cong., 1st Sess. (1866).

47 The committee hoped: Foner, *Second Founding*, 69–70.

48 The court in *Dred Scott*: *Dred Scott v. Sandford*, 60 U.S. 393, 405 (1857).

48 "the great question of citizenship": Cong. Globe, 39th Cong., 1st Sess. 2890 (1866).

48 Repeatedly and publicly, John Bingham: Amar, *America's Constitution*, 387; Meyer, *Amendment That Refused to Die*, 64–66; Foner, *Second Founding*, 75.

49 "free to suppress speech": Michael Kent Curtis, *No State Shall Abridge: The Fourteenth Amendment and the Bill of Rights* (Durham, NC: Duke University Press, 1986), 23.

49 Bingham hoped: Meyer, *Amendment That Refused to Die*, 59.

50 a Virginia law punished: Virginia Code of 1849, Section 22, quoted in Douglas M. Fraleigh and Joseph S. Tuman, *Freedom of Expression in the Marketplace of Ideas* (Los Angeles: Sage, 2011), 44.

50 In Louisiana: Lydia Maria Child, *An Appeal in Favor of That Class of Americans Called Africans* (Boston, 1833), 71.

50 "In Mississippi": Child, *Appeal in Favor of Africans*, 71.

50 "For publishing, or circulating": This and the punishments in Georgia, Louisiana, and Viriginia are from Child, *Appeal in Favor of Africans*, 67.

50 In Tennessee: William Goodell, *The American Slave Code in Theory and Practice Its Distinctive Features Shown by Its Statutes, Judicial Decisions, and Illustrative Facts* (New York, 1853), 386–87.

51 Many southern mail carriers: Fraleigh and Tuman, *Freedom of Expression*, 44.

51 "departures from their own constitutions": Meyer, *Amendment That Refused to Die*, 9.

52 "that quarter where": 1 Annals of Cong. 454–55 (1789).

52 a rule that said: 24 Reg. Deb. 4052 (1836).

52 "Free Speech, Free Press": Rallying song of John C. Fremont, 1856, Library of Congress, hdl.loc.gov/loc.rbc/rbpe.12201000.

52 "But free discussion of the morality": Cong. Globe, 36th Cong., 1st Sess., 2321 (1860).

52 meant to incorporate free speech: Fraleigh and Tuman, *Freedom of Expression*, 46.

52 "make kids feel bad": Statement of Idaho legislator Ron Nate, in "What You Need to Know About Idaho's New Critical Race Theory Law," ABC4, May 4, 2021, www.abc4.com/news/local-news/what-you-need-to-know-about-idahos-critical-race-theory-law/.

53 "By the mid-1870s": Foner, *Second Founding*, 76.

53 "deep and revolutionary": "The Howard Amendment vs. President Johnson's Policy," editorial, *Raleigh Sentinel*, September 19, 1866.

55 Section 2 has never actually been used: Amar, *America's Constitution*, 395; Foner, *Second Founding*, 85.

56 when white women's rights advocates: Foner, *Second Founding*, 81.

58 "transformative" and "to uproot": Amar, *America's Constitution*, 363.

58 the intent of Section 5 was: Meyer, *Amendment That Refused to Die*, 78.

58 "It falls far short": Cong. Globe, 39th Cong., 1st Sess., 2459 (1866).

58 This ultimately convinced: Foner, *Second Founding*, 89.

58 "political privilege granted": Garrett Epps, *Democracy Reborn: The Fourteenth Amendment and the Fight for Equal Rights in Post–Civil War America* (New York: Henry Holt, 2006), 104–5.

58 first Reconstruction Act of 1867: 14 Stat. 428 (1867); Foner, *Second Founding*, 90.

59 "The framers of the Fourteenth": Foner, *Second Founding*, 91.

59 Civil Rights Enforcement Act of 1870: 16 Stat. 140 (1870).

59 The 1870 act clarified: Meyer, *Amendment That Refused to Die*, 65.

61 "indefiniteness of meaning": George S. Boutwell, *Reminiscences of Sixty Years in Public Affairs*, vol. 2 (New York: McClure, Phillips, 1902), 242, quoted in Foner, *Second Founding*, xxv.

Chapter 4

66 "contribution to truth": Ida B. Wells, preface to *Southern Horrors: Lynch Law in All Its Phases* (New York, 1892).

66 "the leading business men, in their leading business centre": Wells, *Southern Horrors*, 5.

67 Indeed, Wells explained: Wells, *Southern Horrors*, 6.

67 728 Black people were lynched: All figures are from Wells, *Southern Horrors*, 14.

67 One woman's confession: "Horrible but True," *Cleveland Gazette*, January 16, 1892, quoted in Wells, *Southern Horrors*, 7.

67 "When the victim is a colored woman": Wells, *Southern Horrors*, 11.

68 were about butchers and livestock: All information about this ruling comes from *Slaughterhouse Cases*, 83 U.S. 36 (1873); Meyer, *Amendment That Refused to Die*, 75–82; and Foner, *Second Founding*, 133–34.

69 "The language is": *Slaughterhouse Cases*, 83 U.S. at 74.

70 *Walker v. Sauvinet*: 92 U.S. 90 (1875).

71 The court reached a similar conclusion: *O'Neil v. Vermont*, 144 U.S. 323 (1892).

71 "and other places of public amusement": Civil Rights Act of 1875, 18 Stat., pt. 3, 335 (1875).

71 But the Supreme Court would overturn: *Civil Rights Cases*, 109 U.S. 3 (1883).

72 "does not authorize Congress": *Civil Rights Cases*, 109 U.S. at 11.

72 "special favorite of the laws": *Civil Rights Cases*, 109 U.S. at 25.

72 *Hall v. DeCuir*: 95 U.S. 485 (1877).

Chapter 5

76 "Under no construction of that provision": *Slaughterhouse Cases*, 83 U.S. at 81.

76 "mediocrities . . . from privileged backgrounds": Foner, *Second Founding*, 129.

77 "The pressure of the growth": Meyer, *Amendment That Refused to Die*, 126.

77 The most important: *Lochner v. New York*, 198 U.S. 45 (1905).

78 "What *Lochner* and its successors": Baer, *Equality Under the Constitution*, 278.

78 the Supreme Court struck down: See *Adkins v. Children's Hospital*, 261 U.S. 525 (1923), and *Hammer v. Dagenhart*, 247 U.S. 251 (1918).

78 *Hurtado v. California*: 110 U.S. 516 (1884).

79 Supreme Court reached: *Maxwell v. Dow*, 176 U.S. 581 (1900).

80 Supreme Court further limited: *Frank v. Mangum*, 237 U.S. 309 (1915). All information about the case comes from the court's decision and Meyer, *Amendment That Refused to Die*, 165–66.

81 "allegation that mob domination": *Frank*, 237 U.S. at 310.

81 "reason to suppose that": *Frank*, 237 U.S. at 333.

Chapter 6

84 "willfully utter, print, write, or publish": Sedition Act of 1918, 40 Stat. 553 (1918).

85 In 1919, white planters and merchants: All information about the Elaine massacre comes from Meyer, *Amendment That Refused to Die*, 169–71.

86 "The Court and neighborhood were thronged": *Moore v. Dempsey*, 261 U.S. 86 (1923), 89–90.

87 *Moore v. Dempsey*: 261 U.S. 86 (1923).

87 "Well—Pitney was gone": Melvin I. Urofsky, "The Brandeis-Frankfurter Conversations," 1985 Sup. Ct. Rev. 299, 316 (conversation of July 3, 1923).

88 Scholars suggest it may have been Bratton's: Meyer, *Amendment That Refused to Die*, 171.

88 "the flux in social consciousness": "Mob Domination of a Trial as a Violation of the Fourteenth Amendment," *Harvard Law Review* 37, no. 2 (Dec., 1923): 250.

88 made the court more sensitive: Meyer, *Amendment That Refused to Die*, 171.

88 "whole proceeding is a mask": *Moore*, 261 U.S. at 91.

88 due process clause protected: *Powell v. Alabama*, 287 U.S. 45 (1932). Specifics about the Scottsboro case come from the court decision; Meyer, *Amendment That Refused to Die*, 189–92; and "ACLU History: Scottsboro Boys," September 1, 2010, American Civil Liberties Union, www.aclu.org/other/aclu-history-scottsboro-boys.

89 "the failure of the trial court": *Powell*, 287 U.S. at 71.

90 The *Lochner* era finally ended: *West Coast Hotel Co. v. Parrish*, 300 U.S. 379 (1937).

91 *Meyer v. Nebraska*: 262 U.S. 390 (1923).

92 "The 'privileges' and 'immunities'": Meyer, *Amendment That Refused to Die*, 178.

92 *Gilbert v. Minnesota*: 254 U.S. 325 (1920) (Brandeis, J., dissenting).

93 "I cannot believe": *Gilbert*, 254 U.S. at 343 (Brandeis, J., dissenting).

93 *Gitlow v. New York*: 268 U.S. 652 (1925).

93 "We may and do assume": *Gitlow*, 268 U.S. at 666.

94 *Mapp v. Ohio*: 367 U.S. 643 (1961).

94 *Gideon v. Wainwright*: 372 U.S. 335 (1963).

94 *Timbs v. Indiana*: No. 17–1091, slip op. (U.S. Sup. Ct. February 20, 2019).

Chapter 7

99 *Plessy v. Ferguson*: 163 U.S. 537 (1896).

102 Massachusetts Supreme Court case: *Roberts v. Boston*, 59 Mass. 198 (1850). All the information about this case comes from the court decision and Meyer, *Amendment That Refused to Die*, 14, 16.

103 "secure for all people": "Our History," NAACP, naacp.org/about/our-history.

104 Working with the NAACP: *Buchanan v. Warley*, 245 U.S. 60 (1917); see also Meyer, *Amendment That Refused to Die*, 152.

104 "the right of the individual": *Buchanan*, 245 U.S. 60 at 80. The court was quoting the Georgia Supreme Court in *Carey v. Atlanta*, 143 Georgia 192 (1915), which struck down a similar law in Georgia.

104 In 1926, the Supreme Court held: *Corrigan v. Buckley*, 271 U.S. 323 (1926).

105 *Shelley v. Kraemer*: 334 U.S. 1 (1948).

107 The court getting involved to enforce: *Shelley*, 334 U.S. at 20.

107 Black people applying for home loans: National Association of Realtors

Research Group, *2023 Snapshot of Race and Home Buying in America* (Washington, D.C.: National Association of Realtors, 2023), 19.

108 "pervasively and deeply embedded": Paula A. Braveman et. al, "Systemic and Structural Racism: Definitions, Examples, Health Damages, and Approaches to Dismantling," abstract, *Health Affairs* 41, no. 2 (February 2022): 171, doi .org/10.1377/hlthaff.2021.01394.

108 "deeply rooted, unfair systems": Braveman, "Systemic and Structural Racism," 172.

108 "An honest assessment": Ta-Nehisi Coates, "The Case for Reparations," *The Atlantic*, June 2014, www.theatlantic.com/magazine/archive/2014/06/the-case -for-reparations/361631/.

109 *Guinn v. United States*: 238 U.S. 347 (1915).

109 "person who was": *Guinn*, 238 U.S. at 357.

109 "How can there be room": *Guinn*, 238 U.S. at 363.

110 Poll taxes persisted until the mid-1960s: *Harper v. Virginia State Board of Elections*, 383 U.S. 663 (1966).

110 Today, states are attacking voting: A periodically updated roundup of state restrictions on voting can be found at the website for the Brennan Center for Justice. Our examples come from the "Voting Laws Roundup" of May 2021, www.brennancenter.org/our-work/research-reports/voting-laws-roundup-may -2021.

111 "was motivated at least": *Holmes v. Moore*, No. 18 CVS 15292, at 101 (N.C. Superior Ct., September 17, 2021). This decision was overturned by the N.C. Supreme Court in 2023, which found that the plaintiffs had "failed to prove beyond a reasonable doubt" that the voter ID law "was enacted with discriminatory intent or that the law actually produces a meaningful disparate impact along racial lines." *Holmes v. Moore*, No. 342PA19–3, at 53 (N.C. Supreme Ct., April 28, 2023).

111 *Murray v. Pearson*: 169 Md. 478, 182 A. 590 (1936).

112 "To attend Howard University": *Murray*, 169 Md. at 488.

112 *Brown v. Board of Education of Topeka*: 347 U.S. 483 (1954).

112 "Witnesses testified that segregation": Oral argument, *Briggs et al v. Elliott et al*, December 9, 1952. https://apps.lib.umich.edu/brown-versus-board-education /oral/Marshall&Davis.pdf.

113 "concerned that destroying all-black schools": Charise Cheney, "Blacks on *Brown*: Intra-Community Debates over School Desegregation in Topeka, Kansas, 1941–1955," *Western Historical Quarterly* 42, no. 4 (Winter 2011): 482, doi.org/10.2307/westhistquar.42.4.0481.

113 "had access to equitable facilities and funding": Cheney, "Blacks on *Brown*," 488.

113 "We conclude that": *Brown*, 347 U.S. at 495.

113 The only difference between: Meyer, *Amendment That Refused to Die*, 222.

115 "were subjected to physical violence": Leslie T. Fenwick, "The Ugly Backlash to *Brown v. Board of Ed.* That No One Talks About," opinion, Politico, May 17, 2022, www.politico.com/news/magazine/2022/05/17/brown-board-education -downside-00032799.

115 "racial prejudice prohibited them": Cheney, "Blacks on *Brown*," 499.

115 "100,000 Black principals": Fenwick, "Ugly Backlash to *Brown*."

115 *Green v. County School Board of New Kent County*: 391 U.S. 430 (1968).

116 *Swann v. Charlotte-Mecklenburg Board of Education*: 402 U.S. 1 (1971).

116 *Milliken v. Bradley*: 418 U.S. 717 (1974).

116 "limited the reach of *Brown*": James Ryan, in "*Brown* at 60 and *Milliken* at 40," *Ed. Magazine*, Harvard Graduate School of Education, June 4, 2014, www.gse.harvard.edu/ideas/ed-magazine/14/06/brown-60-and-milliken-40.

116 A 2022 study: U.S. Government Accounting Office, *K–12 Education: Student Population Has Significantly Diversified, But Many Schools Remain Divided Along Racial, Ethnic, and Economic Lines* (Washington, D.C., June 2022), www.gao .gov/assets/gao-22-104737.pdf.

117 "wanted the world to see": Simeon Wright, "Emmett Till's Casket Goes to the Smithsonian," interview by Abby Callard, *Smithsonian Magazine*, November 2009, www.smithsonianmag.com/arts-culture/emmett-tills-casket-goes-to-the -smithsonian-144696940/.

117 a Belgian newspaper: "The Murder of Emmett Till," timeline, *American Experience*, April 15, 2023, PBS, www.pbs.org/wgbh/americanexperience /features/till-timeline.

117 Just months after their acquittal: William Bradford Huie, "The Shocking Story of Approved Killing in Mississippi," *Look*, January 24, 1956.

117 But it would be another *fifty years*: Carolyn Bryant Donham, interview, September 8, 2008, quoted in Timothy B. Tyson, *The Blood of Emmett Till* (New York: Simon & Schuster, 2017), 7.

117 "Rosa Parks would tell me": Mamie Till-Mobley and Christopher Benson, *Death of Innocence: The Story of the Hate Crime That Changed America* (New York: Random House, 2003), 257.

118 "argued that more was at stake": *Encyclopedia Britannica*, s.v. "Malcolm X," by Lawrence A. Mamiya, last updated July 3, 2023, www.britannica.com /biography/Malcolm-X.

119 *Pace v. Alabama*: 106 U.S. 583 (1883).

120 "Whatever discrimination is made": *Pace*, 106 U.S. at 585.

120 *Loving v. Virginia*: 388 U.S. 1 (1967). The quotes from the court's opinion can be found at 2–3, 8, and 11.

124 *Regents of the University of California v. Bakke*: 438 U.S. 265 (1978).

124 "how difficult it is": Baer, *Equality Under the Constitution*, 18.

125 *Grutter v. Bollinger*: 539 U.S. 306 (2003).

125 *Fisher v. University of Texas*: 579 U.S. 365 (2016).

125 *Students for Fair Admissions, Inc. v. President and Fellows of Harvard College*: 600 U.S. 181 (2023).

125 "Eliminating racial discrimination": *Students for Fair Admissions*, 600 U.S. at 184.

125 "our country has never been colorblind": *Students for Fair Admissions*, 600 U.S. at 385.

126 "by organizing our community": "Who We Are," The Marsha P. Johnson Institute, marshap.org/who-we-are/.

Chapter 8

128 "beyond recognition": Baer, *Equality Under the Constitution*, 106.

129 Myra Bradwell's case: *Bradwell v. The State*, 83 U.S. 130 (1873) (Bradley, J., concurring).

130 upheld an Oregon law: *Muller v. Oregon*, 208 U.S. 412 (1908).

130 the court upheld a Michigan law: *Goesaert v. Cleary*, 335 U.S. 464 (1948).

130 any time a plaintiff brought: Meyer, *Amendment That Refused to Die*, 211.

133 *Reed v. Reed*: 404 U.S. 71 (1971).

135 *Frontiero v. Richardson*: 411 U.S. 677 (1973).

135 *Craig v. Boren*: 429 U.S. 190 (1976).

135 "does not satisfy us": *Craig*, 429 U.S. at 204.

136 *Sessions v. Morales-Santana*: 137 S. Ct. 1678 (2017).

136 encompasses the right to equal protection: *Bolling v. Sharpe*, 347 U.S. 497, 499 (1954).

136 "equal protection analysis": *Buckley v. Valeo*, 424 U.S. 1, 93 (1976).

136 "would care little about": *Sessions*, 137 S. Ct. at 1692, 1696.

136 *Grimm v. Gloucester County School Board*: 972 F.3d 586, 620 (4th Cir. 2020), rehearing denied, 976 F.3d 399 (4th Cir. 2020), cert. denied, 141 S. Ct. 2878 (2021).

137 Other courts have held: See *Hecox v. Little*, 479 F. Supp. 3d 930, 973–75 (D. Idaho 2020) and *Brandt v. Rutledge*, 551 F. Supp. 3d 882, 889–94 (E.D. Ark. 2021); *L.W. et al. v. Skrmetti et al.*, No. 23–5600, (M.D. Ten. 2023); *Eknes-Tucker v. Marshall*, No. 22-CV-184, 2022 WL 1521889, at 13 (M.D. Ala. May 13, 2022).

137 Gender-affirming care "encompasses a range": Patrick Boyle, "What Is Gender-Affirming Care? Your Questions Answered," Association of American Medical

Colleges, April 12, 2022, www.aamc.org/news/what-gender-affirming-care
-your-questions-answered.

138 *Bush v. Gore*: 531 U.S. 98 (2000).

138 "It is no secret": Jack M. Balkin, "*Bush v. Gore* and the Boundary Between Law
and Politics," *Yale Law Journal* 110, no. 8 (June 2001): 1407, www.jstor.org
/stable/797581.

139 Definitions: "Glossary of Terms," Human Rights Campaign, www.hrc.org
/resources/glossary-of-terms.

140 The privacy doctrine began: *Griswold v. Connecticut*, 381 U.S. 479 (1965).

142 Supreme Court extended the right: *Eisenstadt v. Baird*, 405 U.S. 438 (1972).

143 *Roe v. Wade*: 410 U.S. 113 (1973).

143 *Planned Parenthood v. Casey*: 505 U.S. 833 (1992).

144 "the human right to maintain": "Reproductive Justice," SisterSong, www
.sistersong.net/reproductive-justice.

144 *Dobbs v. Jackson Women's Health Organization*: No. 19–1392, slip op. (U.S.
Sup. Ct. June 24, 2022).

144 *June Medical Services v. Russo*: No. 18–1323, slip op. (U.S. Sup. Ct. June 29, 2020).

Chapter 9

146 "more than 2,000 African Americans": https://calisphere.org/exhibitions
/essay/4/gold-rush/.

146 more than twenty thousand: "From Gold Rush to Golden State," Early
California History: An Overview, Library of Congress, www.loc.gov
/collections/california-first-person-narratives/articles-and-essays/early-california
-history/from-gold-rush-to-golden-state/.

148 "every Chinese house": "Reign of Riot," *San Francisco Chronicle*, July 26, 1877.

149 "The Chinese Exclusion Act worked": Gabriel J. Chin, "*Chae Chan Ping* and
Fong Yue Ting: The Origins of Plenary Power," in *Immigration Stories*, ed.
David A. Martin and Peter H. Schuck (New York: Foundation Press, 2005), 8.

149 *Chae Chan Ping v. United States*: Chinese Exclusion Case, 130 U.S. 581 (1889).

150 "open to controversy": This and following excerpt are at *Chinese Exclusion Case*,
130 U.S. at 603, 606.

150 plenary power doctrine defines: Jason H. Lee, "Unlawful Status as a
'Constitutional Irrelevancy'?: The Equal Protection Rights of Illegal Immigrants,"
Golden Gate University Law Review 39, no. 1 (2008), digitalcommons.law.ggu
.edu/ggulrev/vol39/iss1/1.

150 Noncitizens are not guaranteed: *Demore v. Kim*, 538 U.S. 510 (2003).

151 "In immigration court": John Gihon quoted in Gretchen Frazee, "What
Constitutional Rights Do Undocumented Immigrants Have?," *PBS NewsHour*,

June 25, 2018, www.pbs.org/newshour/politics/what-constitutional-rights-do
-undocumented-immigrants-have.

151 "Employ no Mexican": Frost, *You Are Not American*, 162.

151 No one is quite sure: Frost, *You Are Not American*, 165.

152 Approximately 1.5 million: Frost, *You Are Not American*, 171.

152 "they cannot be said": This and following quotes come from Kevin R. Johnson,
"Trump's Latinx Repatriation," *UCLA Law Review* 66 (2019): 1446, 1457,
1464, www.uclalawreview.org/trumps-latinx-repatriation/.

153 *United States v. Wong Kim Ark*: 169 U.S. 649 (1898).

154 "the acts of Congress": *Wong*, 169 U.S. at 653.

154 "mere accident of birth": Attorney George D. Collins, author of U.S.
government brief in *Wong*, quoted in "No Ballots for Mongols," *San Francisco
Examiner*, May 2, 1896, quoted in Frost, *You Are Not American*, 56.

154 "because under international law": Akhil Reed Amar and John C. Harrison,
"The Citizenship Clause: Common Interpretation," National Constitution
Center, constitutioncenter.org/interactive-constitution/interpretation
/amendment-xiv/clauses/700.

155 Wong's lawyers emphasized: Frost, *You Are Not American*, 57–58.

155 "To hold that the Fourteenth Amendment": *Wong*, 169 U.S. at 694.

155 "strangers in the land": *Wong*, 169 U.S. at 731 (Fuller, C.J., Harlan, J., dissenting).

156 "We boast of the freedom": *Plessy*, 163 U.S. at 562 (Harlan, J., dissenting).

156 Wong himself was arrested: Frost, *You Are Not American*, 67.

156 Congress had tried to do the same in 1995 and 2005: Tom Jawetz and Sanam
Malik, "Turning Our Backs on the 14th Amendment," Center for American
Progress, November 9, 2015, www.americanprogress.org/article/turning-our
-backs-on-the-14th-amendment/.

157 *Mackenzie v. Hare*: 239 U.S. 299 (1915).

158 gave Congress a lot of power: Frost, *You Are Not American*, 90.

158 U.S. government had denaturalized: Frost, *You Are Not American*, 151.

158 *Afroyim v. Rusk*: 387 U.S. 253 (1967).

159 "All persons born or naturalized": *Afroyim*, 387 U.S. at 262.

159 fewer than 150 people: Patrick Weil, quoted in Kritika Agarwal, "Stripping
Naturalized Immigrants of Their Citizenship Isn't New," *Smithsonian Magazine*,
July 24, 2018, www.smithsonianmag.com/history/stripping-naturalized
-immigrants-their-citizenship-isnt-new-180969733/.

159 appeared to target: Maryam Saleh, "The Justice Department Singled Out
This Man in Expanding Efforts to Strip Citizenship," The Intercept, February
23 2019, theintercept.com/2019/02/23/denaturalization-operation-janus
-citizenship-trump/.

160 "patriotic citizen": 121 Cong. Rec. 23947 (July 22, 1975) (statement of Rep. Robinson).

161 "to prescribe military areas": Executive Order 9066, February 19, 1942, National Archives, catalog.archives.gov/id/5730250.

162 "the situation in at least some": Harold L. Ickes to President Franklin Roosevelt, April 13, 1943, FDR Library, www.fdrlibrary.marist.edu/_resources /images/sign/fdr_51.pdf.

162 "in a horse stall with a cot": Erick Trickey, "Fred Korematsu Fought Against Japanese Internment in the Supreme Court . . . and Lost," *Smithsonian Magazine*, January 30, 2017, www.smithsonianmag.com/history/fred-korematsu-fought -against-japanese-internment-supreme-court-and-lost-180961967/.

162 *Korematsu v. United States*: 323 U.S. 214 (1944).

162 "because of hostility to him or his race": *Korematsu*, 323 U.S. at 223.

163 In his dissent: *Korematsu*, 323 U.S. at 240–41 (Murphy, J., dissenting).

163 "a level of individualized due process": Frost, *You Are Not American*, 126.

163 "In fact": Richard Reeves, *Infamy: The Shocking Story of the Japanese American Internment in World War II* (New York: Henry Holt, 2015), xiv.

164 "obvious racial discrimination": Justice Murphy's words can be found in *Korematsu*, 323 U.S. at 234–35, 242 (Murphy, J., dissenting).

164 *Yick Wo v. Hopkins*: 118 U.S. 356 (1886).

164 Since then, the Supreme Court has ruled: See *Graham v. Richardson*, 403 U.S. 365 (1971); *Nyquist v. Mauclet*, 432 U.S. 1 (1977); and *Plyler v. Doe*, 457 U.S. 202 (1982).

164 For many undocumented people: Frazee, "What Constitutional Rights."

165 "has been used in support": *Korematsu*, 323 U.S. at 240 (Murphy, J., dissenting).

165 *Trump v. Hawaii*: No. 17–965, slip op. (U.S. Sup. Ct. June 26, 2018).

165 "*Korematsu* has nothing to do with this case": *Trump v. Hawaii*, slip op. at 38.

166 Organized Communities Against Deportation: "Our Story," justicepower .org/project/organized-communities-against-deportation/.

166 California Immigrant Policy Center: "What We Do," caimmigrant.org/what -we-do/.

Chapter 10

167 Michael Hardwick: Information about Hardwick and his arrest comes from William N. Eskridge Jr., *Dishonorable Passions: Sodomy Laws in America, 1861–2003* (New York: Viking, 2008), 230, 232.

167 "jury and military service": Eskridge, *Dishonorable Passions*, 7.

168 "important state symbols": Eskridge, *Dishonorable Passions*, 252.

168 *Bowers v. Hardwick*: 478 U.S. 186 (1986).

168 These terms are defined by: "Glossary of Terms," Human Rights Campaign, hrc.org/resources/glossary-of-terms. Updated 5/31/2023.

170 The district attorney decided: Eskridge, *Dishonorable Passions*, 234.

170 "a fundamental right upon homosexuals": *Bowers*, 478 U.S. at 186.

170 "the infamous crime against nature": *Bowers*, 478 U.S. at 197 (Burger, C.J., concurring), quoting Blackstone's Commentaries IV, 215.

170 The case was not about: *Bowers*, 478 U.S. at 199 (Blackmun, J., dissenting), quoting *Olmstead v. United States*, 277 U.S. 438, 478 (1928) (Brandeis, J., dissenting).

171 "depriving individuals of the right": *Bowers*, 478 U.S. at 214 (Blackmun, J., dissenting).

171 "It was a sign that the Court": Elizabeth Sheyn, "The Shot Heard Around the LGBT World: *Bowers v. Hardwick* as a Mobilizing Force for the National Gay and Lesbian Task Force," *Touro Law Center Journal of Race, Gender, and Ethnicity* 4, no. 1 (May 2009): 2, www.tourolaw.edu/journalrge/uploads/issues/vol4issue1/sheyn-final.pdf.

171 "to approach the bench": Lena Williams, "600 in Gay Demonstration Arrested at Supreme Court," *New York Times*, October 14, 1987, nyti.ms/47gobRz.

171 *Lawrence v. Texas*: 539 U.S. 558 (2003).

171 "To say that the issue in *Bowers*": This and the following quotes from the opinion are from *Lawrence*, 539 U.S. at 567, 578.

172 most Americans in a Gallup poll: Frank Newport, "Six out of 10 Americans Say Homosexual Relations Should Be Recognized as Legal," Gallup News Service, May 15, 2003, news.gallup.com/poll/8413/Six-Americans-Say-Homosexual-Relations-Should-Recognized-Legal.aspx.

173 "was able to establish": Sheyn, "Shot Heard Around the LGBT World," 2.

173 "early gay and lesbian rights advocates": Nancy Polikoff, *Beyond (Straight and Gay) Marriage* (Boston, MA: Beacon Press, 2008), 5.

174 "gay liberation meant something more": William N. Eskridge Jr. and Christopher R. Riano, *Marriage Equality: From Outlaws to In-Laws* (Yale, CT: Yale University Press, 2020), 10.

174 "If other couples have the right to marry": Eskridge and Riano, *Marriage Equality*, 6–7.

174 *Obergefell v. Hodges*: 576 U.S. 644 (2015).

174 "deprived of liberty and property": *Baker v. Nelson*, 291 Minn. 310 (1971). The following quotes from the opinion are found at *Baker*, 291 Minn. at 312, 315.

175 no "substantial federal question": *Baker v. Nelson*, 291 Minn. 310 (1971), cert. denied, 409 U.S. 810 (1972).

176 *United States v. Windsor*: 570 U.S. 744 (2013).

176 "long opposed": Bill Clinton, "Statement on Same-Gender Marriage," September 20, 1996, *Public Papers of the Presidents: William J. Clinton, 1996*, vol. 2 (Washington, D.C.: U.S. Government Printing Office, 1998), 1635.

176 "impose[d] a disadvantage": *Windsor*, 570 U.S. at 770.

178 No union is more profound: *Obergefell*, 576 U.S. at 681.

179 "Although the *Obergefell* decision": Melissa Murray, "*Obergefell v. Hodges* and Nonmarriage Inequality," *California Law Review* 104, no. 5 (October 2016): 1207.

180 "reversing, rather than": Polikoff, *Beyond*, 98.

180 "the framing of marriage": Dean Spade, *Normal Life: Administrative Violence, Critical Trans Politics, and the Limits of Law* (New York: South End Press, 2011), 31.

180 "rules that govern gender classification": Spade, *Normal Life*, 12.

181 *Bostock v. Clayton County*: No. 17–1618, slip op. (U.S. Sup. Ct., June 15, 2020).

181 between 1979 and 2006: Kevin M. Clermont and Stewart J. Schwab, "Employment Discrimination Plaintiffs in Federal Court: From Bad to Worse?" *Cornell Law Faculty Publications*, Paper 109 (2009): 127, https://scholarship .law.cornell.edu/lsrp_papers/109/.

181 Courts have held: Spade, *Normal Life*, 56, citing *Kahakua v. Friday*, 876 F.2d 896 (9th Cir. 1989); *Rogers v. American Airlines*, 527 F Supp. 229 (1981).

182 "chilling effect": Tracie Cone, "Landmark by Design," *Miami Herald*, December 17, 1990, quoted in Eskridge, *Dishonorable Passions*, 264.

182 "entertainment, news, and digital media": "Our Work," GLAAD, www.glaad .org/programs.

182 New Jersey Department of Corrections: "In 2021, Our Fight for LGBTQ Rights Moved to the States," American Civil Liberties Union, December 21, 2021, www .aclu.org/news/lgbtq-rights/in-2021-our-fight-for-lgbtq-rights-moved-to-the-states.

Conclusion

185 "what makes something constitutional": Nikolas Bowie, in Jeannie Suk Gersen, "The Importance of Teaching Dred Scott," *New Yorker*, June 8, 2021, www .newyorker.com/news/our-columnists/the-importance-of-teaching-dred-scott.

185 "In general, law school teaches": Spade, *Normal Life*, 106.

185 "There is a lurking tendency": James Stevenson Ramsey, "Lawyering in the Wake: Theorizing the Practice of Law in the Midst of Anti-Black Catastrophe," *CUNY Law Review* 24, no. 1 (Winter 2021): 21.

Infographic Sources

169 Eskridge, *Dishonorable Passions*, fig. 7.1.

172 Eskridge, *Dishonorable Passions*, fig. 9.1; Gallup, LGBTQ+ Rights, news .gallup.com/poll/1651/gay-lesbian-rights.aspx.

Image Credits

The following images on their corresponding pages were provided with the courtesy of:

7: The White House Historical Association; 8–9: National Archives Catalog; 12, 18: Library of Congress; 21: New York Public Library Digital Collections via Wikimedia Commons; 24: University of Houston Libraries Special Collections, Historic Maps, and Rare Books and Maps Collection; 26: National Portrait Gallery, Smithsonian Institution; acquired through the generosity of an anonymous donor; 30: Library of Congress; 37: The Project Gutenberg EBook of Original Photographs Taken on the Battlefields during the Civil War of the United States, by Mathew B. Brady and Alexander Gardner (This file was produced from images generously made available by the Internet Archive); 43, 44: Library of Congress; 51: Missouri History Museum; 60: Library of Congress; 66: Google Arts and Culture, Wikimedia Commons; 74: Wikimedia Commons; 75: United States Senate, Wikimedia Commons; 80: Collection of the Supreme Court of the United States; 81: Wikimedia Commons; 82: Library of Congress; 85: National Library of Australia, Wikimedia Commons; 86: Butler Center for Arkansas Studies, Central Arkansas Library System; 87 (left): Library of Congress; 87 (right): Wikimedia Commons; 89: National Portrait Gallery, Smithsonian Institution, acquired through the generosity of Elizabeth Ann Hylton; 100, 103: Wikimedia Commons; 114: Library of Congress, New York World-Telegram & Sun Collection; 118: Library of Congress; 121: Getty Images; 128, 131: Wikimedia Commons; 133: Carolina Digital Library and Archives; 134: Wikimedia Commons; 141: Getty Images; 142, 147, 148: California Historical Society; 153: National Archives and Records Administration, Wikimedia Commons; 162: Library of Congress; 163: United States National Archives and Records Administration; 175: Library of Congress, LOOK Magazine Photograph Collection; 177, 178: Getty Images

Index